The New Normal of China's Economy: Connotation and Measurement

By Institute of Quantitative &Technical Economics,
Chinese Academy of Social Sciences
Translated by Wang Pinda

 Paths International Ltd

 中国社会科学出版社
CHINA SOCIAL SCIENCES PRESS

About The Authors

Qi Jianguo, research professor and deputy director of Institute of Quantitative & Technical Economics at Chinese Academy of Social Sciences. He is a doctoral advisor at the Graduate School of Chinese Academy of Social Sciences, a member of the Expert Committee of the Joint Conference on National Strategic Emerging Industries, deputy managing director of Chinese Association of Quantitative Economics, honorary President of the School of Economics and Business at Chongqing Technology and Business University, head researcher of the circular economy evaluation project of Philosophy and Social Sciences Innovation Program at the Chinese Academy of Social Sciences. His research focuses mainly on circular economy, technological innovation, economic analysis and prediction. His works include *Technological Innovation: Reform and Restructuring of the National System*; *Industrial Policy and Economic Growth*; *Research on Technological Progress and Structural Shifts*; *Analysis of the New Economy*; *Theories and Mechanisms of the Modern Circular Economy*; *Knowledge Economy and Management*; *Report on China's Development of Circular Economy*; *Technological Economics and Applications*; *On the Deepening of Labor Theory of Value and Benefit Distribution in the Knowledge Economy*; *On the Acceleration of Change of Economic Development Mode*; *On the Social Welfare Effects of Innovation-driven Development*; *Contextual Analysis of China's "New Normal" Economy*; *Connotation and Mechanism of China's New Normal Economy*; *Circular Economy and Green Development: Calling for the Fourth Technological Revolution*.

Li Wenjun, research professor and Head of the Industrial Technology Office of Institute of Quantitative & Technical Economics at Chinese Academy of Social Sciences, doctoral advisor at the Graduate School of Chinese Academy of Social Sciences, deputy director of the Research Center of Chinese Circular Economy and Environmental Evaluation. His research focuses mainly on finance and circular economy. His works include *Macroeconomic Policies in Financial Crises: Effect Measurement and Exit Mechanism* (2014); *Technical Policies on Strategic Emerging Industries* (2014); *China's Development of Strategic Emerging Industries* (2012); *RMB Exchange Rate and China's International Trade* (2012); *Efficiency and Competitiveness of Commercial Banks* (2008); *Identification and Analysis of China's High-growth Industries* (2006); *Efficiency of the Capital Market* (2004).

Peng Xushu, associate research professor and deputy director of the Industrial Economy Office of Institute of Quantitative & Technical Economics at Chinese Academy of Social Sciences, deputy director of the Research Center of Chinese Circular Economy and Environmental Evaluation, director of China Hi-tech Industry Promotion Society. His research focuses on circular economy and technological innovation. He has participated in Major Projects of the National Social Science Fund, the Science and Technology Supporting Project of the Eleventh Five-Year Plan, and Major Projects of Soft Sciences. His works include *Relationship of Technological Progress and Employment in the United States*; *International Comparative Research on the Private Burden of Higher Education Investments*; *China's Steel Industry: Controlling Exports or Leading the World?*;*Establishing Recycling System of Common Urban Waste*; *Low-Carbon Industrial Composition Based on Technical Economics Analysis*; *Report on China's Development of Circular Economy*.

Wang Hong, assistant research professor of the Industrial Economy Office of Institute of Quantitative & Technical Economics at Chinese Academy of Social Sciences. His research focuses on circular economy and technical economy. His works include *Synergy Effects of Circular Economy: Context, Connotation and*

Mechanism; *Economic Thinking on the Control of PM-2.5 Emissions*; *Theoretical Analysis on Industrial-Agricultural Complex Circular Economy*; *Comparing the Energy Consumption of E-commerce and Traditional Commerce*; *Quantitative Analysis of Water Pricing and Social Welfare in a Circular Economy*. He has participated in "Demonstration and Promotion of Water-saving Industrial and Agricultural Complex Circular Economy in Dingxi, Gansu" under the National Science and Technology Supporting Plan, and "Research on Carbon Circulation and Carbon Sink" under the Circular Economy Development Program of the Twelfth Five-Year Plan. He has participated in the formulation of many circular economy development plans, using material flow analysis to study the resource and environmental impact of economic activity.

Director of the Project Team:

Qi Jianguo, research professor and deputy director of Institute of Quantitative & Technical Economics at Chinese Academy of Social Sciences.

Members of the Project Team:

Li Wenjun, research professor and Head of the Industrial Technology Office of Institute of Quantitative & Technical Economics at Chinese Academy of Social Sciences.

Peng Xushu, associate research professor and deputy director of the Industrial Economy Office of Institute of Quantitative & Technical Economics at Chinese Academy of Social Sciences.

Wang Hong, assistant research professor of the Industrial Economy Office of Institute of Quantitative & Technical Economics at Chinese Academy of Social Sciences.

Abstract: Based on an examination of national and international background, this report analyzes the concept of China's New Normal Economy, emphasizing on its conceptual changes, economic theory foundations and its practical background. This report proposes that China's New Normal Economy is a new "market economy normal" during a time when the eight dividends (namely, the dividends of population, productivity, urbanization, economic structure, reform, resource, environment and net export) gradually shrink or vanish. Under the new normal, economic growth at the past super-high speed under "non-market economy normal" will slow down to ordinary speed under "market economy normal". The slowing down of economic growth would be gradual but irreversible. In order to maintain a stable and continuous economic growth under the new normal, this report provides seven strategic measures, including: comprehensive reform strategy to cope with shrinking reform dividend; information driven development strategy to cope with shrinking productivity dividend; human resource nurturing strategy to cope with shrinking population dividend; circular economy strategy to cope with resource and environmental dividends; substantial urbanization strategy to cope with shrinking urbanization dividend; manufacturing and emerging industries upgrading strategy to cope with shrinking structural dividend; and service and trade improvement strategy to cope with shrinking net export dividend.

Key Words: Economy, New Normal Economy, Economic Growth, Economic Dividend

China's central and local governments are presently formulating the 13th Five-Year Plan for Economic and Social Development. The "New Normal Economy" has become the basis of China's economic planning and regulation in 2015, as well as the starting point of the 13th Five-Year Plan's formulation. The "New Normal Economy" is more than a new jargon; it suggests a milestone moment of transformation over the course of China's economic development. Its essence is a new period of adjustment for the dynamics, structure and mechanism of China's economy, most importantly embodied by a noticeable fall in economic growth. However, China is still undergoing the process of "comprehensive integration of four modernizations", namely industrialization, urbanization, informatization and environmentalization. The country's average income is still at a low level, which means economic development should still be put at top priority. With the economy entering a new normal, the dynamics, environment and conditions that sustained high economic growth in the past 30 years have changed greatly, and some of the factors have undergone fundamental changes. In order to sustain strong and stable economic growth and achieve a higher quality of development, a new developmental environment must be created, new developmental momentums added, new developmental paths explored, and new potentials tapped. To sum up, the country should pursue innovation-driven development.

Contents

About The Authors / iii

Chapter 1 The Practical Implications of the New Normal Economy / 1

Chapter 2 Every Country Has Its Own New Normal / 5

Chapter 3 China's New Normal, Theory of Developmental Stages, and The Shrinking or Vanishing of Growth Dividends / 8

I. The origin of economic growth dividends 8

II. Transformation of development stages and deepening of reforms causes the eight growth dividends to shrink or vanish 11

Chapter 4 Distinguishing Between Normality, Abnormality and the New Normal / 37

I. Normality 37

II. Abnormality 39

III. Transformation between Normality, Abnormality and the New Normal 41

Chapter 5 Policy Measures in the Face of New Normal / 44

I. The comprehensive reform strategy to cope with shrinking reform dividend 44

II. The innovation-driven development strategy to cope with shrinking productivity dividend 49

III. Implementing human resource nurturing strategy to cope with vanishing population dividend 54

IV The circular economy strategy to cope with the vanishing environment dividend 58

V The substantial urbanization strategy to cope with shrinking urbanization dividend 66

VI The manufacturing and emerging industries upgrading strategy to cope with vanishing structural dividend 68

VII The trade in services improvement strategy to cope with shrinking net export dividend 74

References / 80

Chapter 1

The Practical Implications of the New Normal Economy

In early 2009, Bill Gross and Mohamed El-Erian of PIMCO, the largest bond fund in the world, summarized the changes in the world economy, especially those in the rich countries, with the term "new normal", which first appeared in 2002 in the United States. They defined several features of the "new normal" economy: weak economic growth, high unemployment, deleveraging in the private sector, strained public finance, and the transfer of growth momentum and wealth vitality from industrialized economies to emerging ones. Meanwhile, they emphasized that the "new normal" refers to what is *most likely* to happen under the current political and economic circumstance, instead of what *should* happen. Zhang Huilian et al. argues that America's "new normal" of 2002 mainly has two meanings: economic recovery without employment growth, and terrorism becoming more tangible in people's daily life (memory of the September 11 attacks was still fresh at that time). Clearly the "new normal" here is not only a new normal of the economy, but also that of society in general.

In fact, when American scholars coined the term "new normal" in 2002, they feared that threats of terrorism and the "crisis" triggered by the bursting of the economic bubble would become a constant reality. In 2010, Mohamed El-Erian, chief executive of PIMCO, put forward again the concept of "new normal" on the 40th annual meeting of the World Economic Forum in Davos, in order to reflect the low level of world economic growth after the financial crisis of 2007-08. "The crisis was not a mere flesh would, easily health with time. Instead, the crisis cut to the bone," El-Erian said. He believed that the new normal was an inevitable outcome of the previous extraordinary years. The new normal has different manifestations in different sectors, elaborated as follows.

The financial sector. The financial system under the "new normal" means a "lower leverage combined with more government intervention". Finance would be more strictly regulated; capital demand would be higher; the banking system would be more efficient. The post-crisis financial system can no longer simply return to the previous state. Along with the new economic wave driven by information technology and the subsequent housing bubble, financial derivatives were very popular in the 20 years before the crisis. Therefore, the American economy has become highly leveraged with barely any regulation, resulting in unprecedented new changes to the economy. No one could predict the results of these changes, so a lot of beneficiaries of the "new economy" were strongly opposed to any regulation governing the booming innovations of financial derivatives. They thought that additional regulations were not justified because the consequences of those innovations were not yet clear. The "new economy darlings" at that time, including George Soros, adamantly denied the necessity to regulate the excesses of financial innovation. But people realized after the crisis that a major cause of the crisis was the excessive freedom of such innovations. The American government has adopted a "deleveraging" approach to economic recovery, strengthening regulation of the market.

Commerce. Consumer groups and their perceptions have changed under the new normal. Stricter regulation of subprime mortgage has restrained the excessive consumption on credit. The business environment has changed accordingly. Businesses should adapt to the changes in consumption attitudes and patterns, and rethink their strategic position in the new normal.

Macroeconomic situation. Economic recovery in the post-crisis era of "new normal" will be a slow and painful process centered on comprehensive structural adjustments. Benefit structures will be reshuffled, and most Americans will and must gradually adapt to the macroeconomic new normal.

We can see that the term "new normal", in the original American sense, was intended to lower expectations of economic and financial recovery after the crisis. Its tone was pessimistic and resigned. It is not a "new new economy" based on the previous prosperity of the new economy. Instead, it is an adjustment and restoration aimed at the structural imbalance and the myriad of problems that emerged with the bubble. It is worth noting that there are differing opinions regarding the existence of the American "new normal" based on different expectations of the future of the American economy.

Since President Xi Jinping invoked the term during his visit to Henan province in 2014, "new normal" has gained importance and popularity in China. President Xi pointed out in May 2014 that "China's development is still in an important period of strategic opportunities, we must strengthen confidence, starting from the current features of China's development, to adapt to the new normal and maintain a normal state of mind on the strategy." The speech was clearly intended to encourage the nation to bravely face the new normal. President Xi expounded the subject again at the APEC meeting in November 2014, describing the new normal as "the economy has still registered considerable increment albeit the slowdown; economic growth has become more stable and been driven by more diverse forces; the economic structure has been improved and upgraded, heralding a more stable development prospect; the government has vigorously streamlined administration and delegated power, which has further unleashed market vitality." The remarks reflected the President's understanding of the fundamental features of the new normal economy and his expectations of China's future development.

On December 9, 2014, the Central Economic Working Conference called for "a scientific understanding of the current situation, an accurate judgment of future trends, a historical and dialectical approach to the periodical nature of China's economic development, and an accurate grasp of the new normal of economic development", and that "the main logic of China's current and future economic development is to recognize, adapt to and lead the new normal". The "new normal" has become the starting point of China's economic reform and development policies. The Central Economic Working Conference analyzed the new features of the Chinese economy from the following eight aspects: consumption, investment, exports and international balance of payment, production capacity and industrial organization mode, production factors, market competition, resource and environment, and economic risks. The Conference conducted the most comprehensive and authoritative analysis and definition of "new normal" so far, and clarified different interpretations of the term that had emerged previously.

In view of the economy's performance in those eight aspects, the Conference stated that the direction of China's economic development would lead to a more advanced shape, a more sophisticated division of labor, and a more reasonable structure. The economy would undergo a shift from high speed growth to a medium-to-high one, from focusing on quantity and speed to quality and efficiency in growth model, from stressing production expansion to improving current production, and from growth being driven by conventional engines to increasingly driven by new ones. These judgments about growth trends are more of an expectation and policy orientation than an inevitable outcome of the "new normal".

Both America and China have put forward the concept of "new normal" based on the reality of socioeconomic development. However, there is still no theoretical or scholarly explanations of the new normal as of now.

Chapter 2

Every Country Has Its Own New Normal

In his article *Raising Quality and Efficiency to Adapt to The New Normal*, Li Yang pointed out that the world economy has entered a period of slowing growth focused on long-term structural adjustment. As the world economy is increasingly integrated, no country can isolate itself from the negative impacts of any economic crisis. After the 2008 crisis, China, starting in 2009, mobilized the strength of the entire state to stimulate the economy with a stimulus package of 4 trillion yuan. The administrative measure did prevent the Chinese economy from the shock that the world economy suffered, and stopped the economy from a precipitous fall in growth. But since 2011 China's macroeconomic growth has slowed nonetheless. There were even signs of crisis in real estate and several other sectors.

Changes from both the supply side and the demand side have shaped the "new normal" of economic development. However, China's "new normal" has essential differences with rich countries in its external form as well as its formation mechanism. Therefore, the new normal economy after the financial crisis has different connotations according to the unique situations of different countries.

In the case of China, economic growth has slowed since 2011; the hard constraint of resource and environment has become even harder; the "three carriages" of economic growth (investment, consumption and net export) are losing steam. Will those features persist in the long term? If so, China will bid farewell to the previous model of cyclical high-speed growth, with the average growth rate lowering from 10% to around 7%. But how long will the new speed last? How long will the normal be? Will China return to the "old normal" of high speed growth of 10% after a period of "new normal" of 7%? And will the American economy return to the "old normal" of medium or even high speed growth cycles after the "new normal" of economic downturn? The new normal has different economic meaning for China and America, because China's present economic downturn and the American recovery after the crisis are not of the same nature.

The Chinese academia is divided on these issues. We believe that it is not theoretically sound or practically meaningful to define the new normal as "the economy has shifted gear from the previous high speed to a medium-to-high speed growth; the economic structure is constantly improved and upgraded; the tertiary industry and consumption demand are becoming the main driver. urban-rural and regional disparities are narrowing; household income is going up as a percentage of national income; the benefits of development are reaching more people; the economy is increasingly driven by innovation instead of input and investment." This description is more of a policy orientation and expectation of the government, rather than a set of benchmarks for the "new normal" economy. Some economists think that "the Chinese economy has shifted to a period of 'normal growth' after 30 years of high speed growth". The statement implies that the present growth rate of 7% to 8% is the "normal" rate. But there is no evidence to back this claim. Why does the normal rate have to be 7% to 8%? Where is the supporting evidence? And what does this "normal" rate have to do with the new normal? How many years did the United States achieve a 7-8% growth rate in its economic history? In fact, a growth rate of 7% to 8% is abnormally high for any mature market economy. Then why should it be the "normal" growth rate for China? Is "normal economic growth" related to the natural growth rate or the potential rate? We need to theoretically and practically answer these questions in order to determine what China's new normal is.

Looking at the growth rates and patterns of many countries in history, we can see that each country had its unique developmental features in different stages of development, but they shared some common characteristics as well. A general rule is that economic growth tends to be higher when a country is undergoing industrialization, and growth begins to slow when industrialization is in its later stages or near or after its completion. Therefore, both the high speed in industrialization periods and the low speed in post-industrialization period are the "normal" of the respective development stages. And each country has its own normal according to its size, history, development stage, resource endowments, and status in the global economic system. The so-called "new normal", therefore, occurs when the environment or stage of economic development changes and the features of economic development move from one equilibrium to another. And these features of development can be expressed with different indicators according to different subjects. Thus the new normal is not uniform around the globe.

Chapter 3

China's New Normal, Theory of Developmental Stages, and The Shrinking or Vanishing of Growth Dividends

It is believed that the causes of China's economic downturn and lack of growth momentum are as follows: overcapacity in production, ecological decay and pollution, slow growth of domestic demand, structural imbalances, lagging external demand and trade imbalances, high income inequality, etc. But we believe that these are immediate causes, not fundamental ones. According to development economics and economic management theories, there are only two fundamental causes. Firstly, the economy has entered a period of transformation. Secondly, the economic reforms that were meant to correct the distorted economic system has shifted the growth momentum away from non-market and towards market-oriented ones. Those two reasons can be explained by the theory that the transformation of developmental stages shrinks economic growth dividends.

I. The origin of economic growth dividends

Economic growth dividends refer to the internal and external factors that exist in an economic system and spontaneously engender economic growth in a specific development stage. In traditional economic theories, there are three major internal factors that fuel economic growth: labor force, capital, and productivity. Changes in those three factors generate economic growth dividends. Labor force is affected by reproductive culture and economic development, and in turn affects economic growth. Capital is the core factor in industrialization, with its effect manifested in quantity, structure and technology levels. Productivity is determined by the quality and structure of the labor force and is also related to the level of technology. It affects economic growth mainly through total factor productivity (TFP), and determines a country's international competitiveness and trade balance. In different stages of development, the three factors have different impacts on economic growth, and the growth dividends change accordingly.

Developmental economics dictates that labor force and capital factors are dominant in the take-off or early industrialization stage of development. With the further progression of industrialization, multiple forces slow down population growth and greatly change the demographics. The population ages, the dependency ratio rises, and the demographic dividend shrinks or even vanishes.

Primitive capital accumulation is lacking in the early stage of industrialization, which means that the strongest impact on economic growth is realized through capital investment on traditional industrialization infrastructure and the development of reproducible heavy industries of scale, bringing the industrial structure dividend that is beneficial to economic growth. The main function of capital in this stage is to develop the capacity of massive industrial production, employ the surplus labor, raise rapidly the household income, and drive economic growth through increasing demand. However, when industrialization is near completion, the markets for industry infrastructure and real estate are almost saturated. The pillars of the industrial economy will stop growing. Rising rate of savings creates a surplus of capital, which blunts the effect of capital on economic growth.

The effect of productivity growth on economic growth is more sustained.

However, factors that raises productivity vary with different development stages. For open developing countries, there is a significant technological disparity with developed countries in the early and middle stages of industrialization, and the prime industries that drives growth are traditional ones with reproducible production capacity. Therefore, production capacity can be developed, labor productivity can be raised, and rapid economic growth can be achieved as long as those developing countries create a market large enough for traditional sectors, import advanced technology from rich countries, make full use of surplus agricultural labor, and duplicate production lines that fit economies of scale. When industrialization is nearly completed, the markets for traditional industries reach saturation, and the growth of demand in those sectors slows down or grinds to a halt. At this time, technological innovation is needed in order to further drive economic growth, for example by developing new technology, new products or even entire new industries. Previously the economy could reap technological import dividend and product export dividend from its disparity with rich countries. But those dividends are gone at the more advanced stages of development. Countries at these stages, as a result, must follow the lead of rich countries to pursue productivity gains through "indigenous technological innovation", which puts these countries in direct competition with rich countries.

It is a pattern of innovation that high risks of failure occur along with the increased productivity brought about by new technologies, new products and new industries, and that the process of knowledge accumulation and human capital formation is vital. The practice of rich countries showed that innovation per se does not necessarily result in a sustained and significant growth in productivity. That is because productivity growth will slow or even stop if the rate of technological innovation cannot keep pace with population growth.

There are also factors that directly affect economic growth outside of the economic system itself. For instance, natural resources are abundant and economic growth requires relatively little input of resources at early stages of industrialization. Therefore, there is a growth dividend in the relatively low prices of natural resources needed for economic growth. Furthermore, the early-stage economy generates relatively little waste and emission, which is below the capacity of natural self-purification. This results in a environmental dividend of economic growth. With the progression of industrialization, the economy becomes larger, consumes more resources, and generates more wastes and emissions. The environmental dividend is then gone.

As China's developmental stage transforms from early-stage industrialization to middle-to-later stages, the Chinese economy also shifts from the sustained high level of growth in the past 30 years towards the present "new normal". At the same time, growth dividends are shrinking or vanishing in the second round of deepening reforms.

II. Transformation of development stages and deepening of reforms causes the eight growth dividends to shrink or vanish

(i) The vanishing population dividend

According to the two-gap model and the dual economy model of development economics, developing countries at the early stages of industrialization have surplus labor due to capital and foreign exchange shortages. In 1978, China started the strategy of Reform and Opening Up, launching the world's largest industrialization process. In the 20 years after 1978, China's most lacking production factors are capital and foreign exchange for importing advanced technology and equipments. The dual gaps of investment and foreign exchange were evident at that time. Furthermore, China's birth rate stayed high from the 1950s to the late 1970s. The population was young and the dependency ratio was steadily declining. Compared with the limited capital investment and foreign exchange reserves, there is almost unlimited supply of labor, mainly young workers suitable for labor-intensive industries, creating the "population dividend" of China's economic growth. In a dual economy, the unlimited supply of rural young workers means that they have almost no negotiating power in the wage decision process. Low cost of labor became the defining feature of China's economy in the past 30 years, allowing the country to achieve rapid growth by attracting foreign investment and turning high savings rate into high levels of domestic investment. The population dividend can be measured by the dependency ratio. "Research models show that every percentage of decrease in the dependency ratio brings a 0.115% increase in per capita growth rate. The declining dependency ratio contributed 27% of China's per capita economic growth. We can consider this as the contribution of the population dividend to China's economic growth."

In 1980, China adopted and now continues to implement the strictest birth control policy of human history. The policy reduced the number of births by 300-400 million in the ensuing 30 years, radically changing the demographic structure and gradually erasing the population dividend. The year 2004 was the first marking point of China's changing population dividend. That winter, China experienced its first shortage of migrant workers. "Migrant workers are the main source of 'unlimited supply' of cheap labor in China. However, since the start of 2004, significant shortages of migrant workers have occurred." Netease News covered the phenomenon with the title "China experienced its first migrant worker shortage in 20 years", saying that "This is the first time in 20 years that employers have to compete for even a single migrant worker. It illustrates the pressing need for free movement of labor, and underlines the rights of those workers. It forces us to rethink the true meaning of China's 'unlimited cheap labor'."

The labor shortage of 2004 marked the start of changes in the population dividend, spurring the academia and the government to recognize the problems of China's labor market. However, the labor shortages at that time were not caused by a decreasing supply of labor. "The labor shortage starting in the spring of 2004 were structural but not comprehensive, national but not regional, and caused by expanding demand but not shrinking supply. The causes of labor shortages include low wages, squalid working conditions, rising agricultural returns, investment stimulus, and changes in demographic structures of the labor force." Since the Asian financial crisis of 1997, China has adopted macroeconomic policies with a goal of 8% growth rate and begun to stimulate the economy, in order to keep the economy growing and withstand the external shocks of economic crises. After three years of effort, China's growth rate started rising again in 2000 to 8.4%. In 2003, China's growth rate again reached double digits. But there are two distinctive features of the round of economic growth starting in 2003.

First, exports in labor-intensive industries skyrocketed after China joined the WTO in 2001. China's total exports of goods grew by 34.66% in 2003 and 35.32% in 2004. The demand for labor by export industries began rising sharply.

Second, domestic demand was largely fueled by industries like infrastructure, real estate and chemicals, further increasing demand for labor.

Just as labor demand kept rising, the effect of the birth control policy on labor supply began to materialize in 2004. Migrant workers, who were always in a disadvantaged position in wage negotiations, now can make their own choices for the first time: if their employers keep suppressing wages, they can vote with their feet. From 2000 to 2010, China's labor force grew by only 13.13%, while the economy grew by 143%, eleven times the growth rate of labor force. Since 2010, labor force growth has slowed further still. In 2013, the number of prime-age workers (16-59 years old) decreased by 2.44 million, marking China's first ever labor force decrease. The number decreased by a further 3.71 million in 2014. "China's labor force will stop growing by 2015 and will begin declining afterwards. The population dividend will disappear. The demographic changes are an inevitable trend of economic and social development. It is irreversible even with changes of birth control policies," predicted Cai Fang of Chinese Academy of Social Science in 2010.The decline came faster than he expected. The decreasing number of prime-age workers means that there will be a shortage of labor supply, pushing up wages. The labor-intensive export industries that have propelled China's growth for so many years will be less competitive because of rising labor costs, leading to lower growth or even shrinking of exports. This is one of the main reasons why China's economy is shifting from high growth to low-to medium growth. The vanishing population dividend means that China will not cyclically recover from low growth to the "old normal" of double-digit growth as it did before. Slowing economic growth will become the new normal.

(ii) The vanishing industrial structure dividend

The propellant of China's high economic growth before 2010 came from not only the population dividend, but also the large scale of investment in the peaking stage of industrialization. China's infrastructure was underdeveloped, investments were needed everywhere, and the country was in an era of long-term relative shortage of capital. Per capita living space was also small. Urban residents had only an average of 7 m^2 of living space in 1978 and 20 m^2 in 2000. China launched a large scale commercialization of the real estate sector in 2002, scrapping the previous welfare housing system whereby people were allocated public housing from the government. Demand of real estate boomed, and prices have risen fast. Investment in both real estate and infrastructure skyrocketed. The automobile sector saw a significant increase in investment after the car boom in 2003. Manufacturing investment grew along with exports. Those four rising investment demands further spurred an increase in demand and prices of heavy industry products, pushing up overall price levels. Real estate price increased 6 to 10 times in different areas in 10 years. In this context, there was a national investment spree in infrastructure, real estate, automobile and commodities like steel and energy. Economic growth accelerated, and inflation soared. In order to prevent the overheating of the economy, the government introduced heavy-handed macroeconomic interventions in 2003, strictly restricting investment and credit in heavy industries such as steel, electricity, aluminum, cement, chemicals and petrol. The government also halted approval of large-scale, technology-intensive projects. However, rising market prices continued to induce local governments and businesses to circumvent administrative control and continue adding investments.

Government-led investment mainly relied on foreign capital, domestic debt, land sales, high business taxes, extra-budgetary charges, and compulsory sales of foreign exchanges. Private sector investment, on the other hand, relied on credit, underground finance, and resource exploitation that damaged the environment.

The combination of intensive investment by governments (local governments in particular) and businesses resulted in an economic growth model whose characteristics included high investment, high exports, high environmental damages, low wages and costs. Before 1996, this model was compatible to the shortages in the domestic market and the high growth in exports. Supported by rising market demand, the economy consistently grew by double digits despite stagnant wages and severe environmental damages. After the adjustment period of 1997-2002 following the Asian crisis, investment strength and high domestic demand joined forces again in 2003-10, bringing about another period of double-digit growth.

The economy was at the early stages of industrialization in the years before 2008, which had the basic features of high capital return, high level of pollution, low wages resulting from the population dividend, and low inclusiveness of economic growth. Most workers did not reap comparable gains from economic development. Macroeconomic regulation at that time mainly included cyclical administrative measures to constrain investment and curb inflation.

However, there were already signs of change in 2004-08. The economy was reaching the middle stages of industrialization, industrial structure was becoming heavier, the population dividend was shrinking, and labor costs were rising. However, the export dividend brought by WTO was materializing. The growing push of net export was able to offset the negative impact of the shrinking population dividend. Although high capital return was still an important feature in this period, rising labor costs increased the inclusiveness of economic growth. And although pollution was growing, efforts to curb it was also gaining momentum, resulting in a tug of war between pollution and conservation. Meanwhile, the contribution of net export to economic growth reached a historical peak. Compared with the years before 2004, rising wages put increasing pressure on businesses, and capital intensity was growing fast. Investment-to-GDP ratio rose further, along with the production capacity of traditional heavy industry sectors. This paved way for excess capacity, falling asset prices, and distorted industrial structure. More unfortunately, policymakers at that time mistakenly predicted the global economic situation and persisted in the habitual thinking of the central-planned economy. As a result, macroeconomic regulations continued to aim at constraining investment and curbing inflation.

From the start of the 2008 global financial crisis till 2013, China's economic regulations focused on combating the negative impacts of the crisis and preventing a steep fall of economic growth. However, by 2008 the economy had already begun to show some signs of later stages of industrialization. The external shock of the financial crisis should have provided an opportunity of structural adjustment and upgrade in order to adapt to the shift in development stages. But policymakers, in their habitual central-planning thinking, still rolled out the 4-trillion-yuan stimulus package even as industrial structures were highly distorted and production capacities were in severe excess. The government even relaxed approvals for the previously restricted projects in the steel sector, such as the Zhanjiang steel project which obtained approval from the National Development and Reform Commission. This kind of blind and reactive stimulus exacerbated the problems of structural distortion and excess capacity.

Since 2005, in fact, China's investment structure has shifted from heavy industry and real estate towards manufacturing, emerging industries and services. As Table 1 shows, the seven commodity-based heavy industries and real estate made up 45.5% of total fixed assets investment in 2005. That proportion has decreased by 5.3% to 40.2% by 2013. Table 2 shows the changes in investments of eight manufacturing and electronics sectors. It shows that the proportion of investments in these sectors shot up from 12.15% of total fixed assets investment in 2005 to 17.37% in 2013, an increase of 5.12%. This is a sign that the market had already started to adjust its industrial structure, but the central government failed to notice this transformative information in its regulatory decision-making.

After thirty years of industrialization and more than a decade of urbanization,

China's economy has entered the middle-to-late stages of industrialization and urbanization. The accumulation of production capacities in traditional sectors, such as real estate and energy-consuming commodity-based heavy industries, has provided ample foundation for industrialization and urbanization. The changes in investment structure in Table 1 and 2 indicates an end of the "extensive" mode of growth that features economies of scale, and that a transition of development stages has begun. The context of this transition is that population growth has slowed and the population dividend gradually vanishes; that the market for basic consumer goods has reached saturation; that the growth in infrastructure has slowed; and that growth in both rigid and improvement demand for real estate has also begun its decline. Those signs show that China's economic development stage is undergoing an essential transformation. Demand in the mass-scale reproducible industries that previously propelled growth, such as steel, heavy industries, automobile and construction, are inching towards saturation. The wave of growth in consumer demand has also subsided. Market demand has begun shifting toward the services sector. The pillar industry that supports growth is moving from heavy industries towards emerging sectors and services. Structural changes in demographics, trade and demand has induced structural changes in investment, bringing down growth rate of investment in heavy industries and real estate while increasing demand for investment in emerging sectors. However, emerging sectors rely heavily on innovation and carry high risks. It needs the accumulation of knowledge and technological innovation, as well as a corresponding set of new commercial and services pattern. Its investment demand will not undergo "extensive" growth like the traditional sectors once did. As the services sector gains weight, growth in labor productivity will fall and investment returns will converge. This transition means that the old structural dividend of economic growth pretty much vanishes.

Table 1 Investment in 8 traditional sectors as a proportion of total fixed assets investment

	2013	2010	2007	2006	2005
Total fixed assets investment (billion yuan)	43574.7	24379.8	11746.4	9336.9	7509.5
1. Real estate	11138.0	5763.3	2861.9	2158.6	1709.8
2. Paper-making	263.6	146.4	221.6	64.7	54.9
3. Petrochemicals and nuclear fuel	303.9	203.5	141.5	93.9	80.1
4. Chemicals manufacturing	1321.0	704.0	353.4	254.0	213.1
5. Ferrous metals	509.9	336.9	261.7	228.5	230.5
6. Non-ferrous metals	555.0	283.0	129.6	96.3	76.1
7. Electricity, gas and water	1962.9	1135.6	908.9	826.1	728.7
8. Mining	1464.9	969.5	525.6	415.3	323.4
Sum	17519.2	9542.2	5264.2	4134.7	3416.6
Proportion of total fixed assets investment (%)	40.20	39.1	44.82	44.31	45.50

Table 2 Investment in manufacturing and electronics as % of total fixed assets investment

	2013	2007	2006	2005
Total fixed assets investment (billion yuan)	43574.7	11746.4	9336.9	7509.5
1. Rubber and plastics	524.7	129.8	107.0	67.6
2. Metal products	713.7	158.0	110.1	74.5
3. Non-metal mineral products	1375.7	280.6	185.6	139.4
4. General-purpose equipment	1049.1	233.1	156.7	102.5
5. Special-purpose equipment	1001.7	168.9	108.9	78.5
6. Electric machines	921.1	160.8	111.1	77.1
7. Transportation equipment	1205.3	272.3	196.7	157.7
8. Electric appliances, communication equipment, computer and other electronic devices	1780.9	398.3	302.3	214.8
Sum	7570.5	1801.8	1278.4	912.1
Proportion of total fixed assets investment (%)	17.37	15.34	13.69	12.15

(iii) The shrinking productivity dividend

Productivity and population growth are the two basic factors that determine economic growth. China's declining population growth is a given factor, and is projected to last for a long time. Therefore, productivity growth becomes the dominant factor affecting economic growth rate. Productivity is determined by many factors, such as quality of the labor force, speed of technological progress, and the compatibility of relations of production and the level of production forces.

The dominant factor affecting productivity growth is different for countries at different development stages. For China, the dominant factor is the improving compatibility between relations of production and level of productive forces brought about by technological and institutional innovations after the Reform and Opening Up. However, the productivity dividend driven by those two factors are now shrinking.

a. Transition of technological innovation finds it hard to accelerate productivity growth

The fundamental source of economic growth is technological innovation and its ensuing productivity growth. In the long term, the speed of innovation is determined by the rate of return for the innovators. The relations of production determine whether the benefit distribution is reasonable and whether the innovator gets sufficient economic return from his innovation. Appropriate relations of production induce rational actors to pursue technological innovation and accelerates its development, and vice versa.

Technological innovation is achieved by improvements or even a revolution of production and management technology which facilitates a rise of productive and factor distributive efficiency, resulting in a positive productivity growth. Rising productivity can be expressed mathematically as a positive second derivative of yield against input, and physically as a positive acceleration rate. If productivity level stays the same, *ceteris paribus*, the productivity growth rate is zero, and long-term economic growth rate would also be zero. Similarly, a slowing productivity growth portends slowing economic growth.

In production, technological innovation means that new technology reduces the amount of input for the same yield, or new products create more utility and market value with the same amount of input, thereby raising productivity growth and economic growth. However, if productivity is merely growing but the growth rate is not accelerating, economic growth will lack acceleration as well. Similarly, if productivity growth rate falls, the economy will continue to grow, but more slowly.

In management, technological innovation means an improvement of the deployment of production factors, strengthening the incentive of the human factor, raising the efficiency of productive innovation. This improves the efficiency of resource and production factors utilization, leading to economic growth. Here the same problem of decelerating growth exists.

From the technical perspective, there are two main sources of production and management innovation: (1) research and development within the economy; (2) introduction of new technology from outside the economy. The rules of technological innovation dictate that research and development of new technology and its application within the economy relies on progress and knowledge, which requires accumulation of time, effort, human capital and R&D investments, carrying various risks of failure. For countries at the forefront of technology, their innovation mainly comes from internal research and development, which is subject to cyclical fluctuation of progress in basic sciences and technology. This means their economic growth also fluctuates cyclically. From the long-term historical perspective, the growth rate of economies based on such "original innovation" relies on the speed of technological innovation. Innovation of those forefront countries has not led to accelerating growth of productivity in macroeconomic terms. Therefore, the growth rate of these economies is also not accelerating. The economic history of rich countries show that their growth has always been fluctuating, without consistent acceleration. This phenomenon can be seen as a rule applied to economies whose growth relies on endogenous innovation based on internal R&D.

Since the beginning of the 21st century, the relationship of China's economic growth and R&D expenditure has shown similar pattern with rich countries. China's R&D spending was only 0.9% of GDP in 2001. In 2014 the figure was 2.1%. According to statistics from the Ministry of Science and Technology (MOST), China's R&D spending in 2014 amounted to 1,340 trillion yuan, 76% of which was made by businesses. At 3.8 million, China also has the world's largest number of full-time R&D personnel. Data from the third national economic census show that the number of businesses involved in R&D has grown twofold. In 2013, 14.8% of above-scale industrial businesses conducted R&D activities, an 8.3% increase from 2008. The quality and quantity of patent applications is rising. Patent and invention applications rose by 223.2% and 368.7% respectively during 2008-13. Applications of patents of invention made up 36.6% of all applications, an increase of 11.4% compared to 2008.

China's R&D spending has grown by twice the GDP growth rate for 13 consecutive years. However, the spectacular achievements in R&D did not crystalize into faster growth of total factor productivity (TFP), suggesting that China is entering a stage of declining productivity growth. Scholars have different analyses of the reason behind this, but their conclusions are largely the same.

The Institute of Quantitative & Technical Economics at Chinese Academy of Social Sciences used traditional quantitative methods and new methods recommended by MOST to calculate the contribution of technological progress to economic growth. The results suggest that the contribution of technological progress (measured in TFP) has declined in 2000-12. Traditional quantitative methods show that the contribution rate was 43.89% in 2000-07, and 20.15% in 2008-12 after the financial crisis. And technological progress (TFP) was declining by 0.41% per year during 2008-12. Using MOST's new method which factors R&D's contribution into productivity, the results show that the contribution rate was 44% in 2000-07 and 43.5% in 2008-12. Although the new method yielded smaller difference before and after the crisis, it still indicates a downward trend.

Contradictory to the relationship between economic growth and internal

R&D-driven innovation, some "catch-up" countries import new knowledge and technology on a massive scale for industrialization, and achieved sustained high economic growth or even accelerating growth. That is the case when Japan implemented the "income-doubling plan" in the 1960s and the Four Asian Tigers introduced technologies and industries from rich countries after the 1970s. In the 30 years up to 2008, China also benefited from massive importation of advanced technology, achieving import-driven technological innovation and sustained high economic growth.

This does not mean that domestic R&D spending has no contribution to economic growth. Instead, China's economic growth would have slowed down earlier or even fall into the middle-income trap if the rapid growth of domestic R&D had not taken place. Since the beginning of this century, active innovation played an important role in increasing China's international competitiveness and catching up with rich countries. However, economic rules and technological rules are different: innovation can guard the economy against sudden slumps but cannot guarantee accelerating growth.

Generally speaking, in the stage of import-driven innovation, the wider the gap between technology exporting and importing countries, the greater the effect of foreign technology on productivity growth of importing countries. However, because the cost of importing technology is classified in economics as fixed assets investment, this kind of productivity growth and its ensuing economic growth is often classified as a contribution of fixed assets investment, or even lamented as an "extensive" way of investment-driven economic growth. But it is important to note that, regardless of those theoretical classifications, import-driven innovation and economic growth saved a great deal of time of R&D by importing existing mature technology systems. Furthermore, it avoided the market uncertainties and risks of researching and developing new technology from scratch. Investment in advanced technology can quickly materialize into mass-scale reproducible production capacity, easily leading to high economic growth.

However, with the rising level of economic development, China's own R&D

ability is also growing, and its technology level is increasingly near the forefront. The time is gone when China could import advanced technology to achieve industry upgrading and mass-scale production capacity, rapidly raise productivity, and supply low-cost products to the market to fuel high economic growth. There are mainly four reasons for this.

Firstly, the cost of domestically producing technological equipment in some fields, especially in traditional manufacturing sectors, is low enough that China no longer needs to buy whole sets of equipment, and is even able to export said equipment in large quantities. There is no further room for economic growth through importing technology. Secondly, the domestic market was previously in a situation where demand exceeded supply. But now domestic supply exceeds demand. There is a market constraint on model of economic growth driven by technology importation and reproduction of capacities. Thirdly, the export market has slowed due to rising costs and stagnant world economy, making it difficult to import technology used for export industries. Fourthly, some core competitive technology is subject to monopolistic embargos and restrictions by rich countries, which has become increasingly difficult to purchase.

Because of those four reasons, the growth of China's goods and processing import has been consistently lower than export since China joined the WTO in 2001. A large trade surplus, high domestic savings and rising domestic demand pushed China prematurely into an era of capital surplus. With the dividend of imported technology shrinking, even the growing internal innovation cannot surpass the rule that developed countries' productivity growth cannot consistently accelerate. It has thus become inevitable that the growth of productivity, TFP and GDP would fall.

b. A rising service sector exerts a downward pressure on productivity growth

There is significant difference in the mechanism and extent of technology absorption among agriculture, industry, construction and services.

In agriculture, a labor-intensive sector, although technological innovation does have a sustained supporting impact on its growth, agriculture ultimately depends more on fundamental resource conditions such as land and climate. Worldwide experience shows that agriculture absorbs modern science and technology very slowly. In China in particular, the land condition is far from ideal. The state of the current land system, based on "household contract responsibility", means that agriculture will remain a labor-intensive sector in the foreseeable future, making it difficult to raise productivity quickly. Even if future land reforms can increase the scale of agricultural production, growth in productivity would still struggle. It is an inevitable trend that agricultural growth will slow down.

Industry does not rely much on land and climate. Sustained progress in science and technology benefits foremost from the absorption of innovation by the manufacturing sector. Industrial manufacturing has developed from manual workshops of yore to today's smart manufacturing, with machines replacing labor and computers replacing the human brain. Smart robots are continually replacing human from the scene of manufacturing, up to the point where humans are completely away from the scene in an unmanned factory. This is the inevitable result of technological progress and roundabout production. Manufacturing is the sector that is most affected by innovation and is able to raise productivity most quickly. Therefore, in the process of structural changes, productivity growth increases along with industrial manufacturing as a proportion of GDP, and vice versa. Since 1990, the contribution of industrial manufacturing to GDP has risen before eventually going down. It stood at 39.7% of GDP in 1990, reached the peak of 62.8% in 1994 before falling to 57.6% in 2000, 48.5% in 2010, 39.9% in 2013, and 35.8% in 2013, even lower than that in 1990. This is also an inevitable trend given that the industrialization process nearing completion, lowering productivity growth.

Building industry is a labor-intensive sector as well. Its contribution to GDP was only 1.3% in 1990, rising to 5.3% in 1994, 3.2% in 2000, 8.3% in 2010, 8.4% in 2013, and falling to 6.8% in 2014, but still much higher than in 1990. In the middle-to-late stages of industrialization, the weight of construction in GDP would stabilize. Although automation in the construction sector is rising in the past years, many construction processes still cannot be automated, especially regarding decoration. Therefore, its productivity will be hard to accelerate.

The service sector produces value directly by labor. It is a labor-intensive sector as well. Services' contribution to GDP was only 17.3% in 1990, rising to 25.5% in 1994, 34.8% in 2000, 39.3% in 2010, 46.8% in 2013, 48.2% in 2014. Actually, the weights of service and manufacruring industry have been mostly on a par since 2001, when service for the first time exceeded manufacturing as a share of GDP. In 2001-11, the two sectors crisscrossed each other. But in 2012-14, service as a share of GDP began to significantly outweigh that of manufacturing. In 2014 the gap was 12.4%.

70%-80% of the service sector exists for the purpose of production. Production-oriented services are knowledge-intensive, such as modern finance, insurance, R&D, technical and informational consulting, knowledge promotion and education. These sectors have a high productivity and constitute an important part of the "new economy". Their development relies on the development of the manufacturing sector, which has high productivity but lower productivity growth. Those service sectors have high added-value and productivity. As their share of GDP grow, the total productivity will grow as well. However, the increase of these sectors as a share of GDP is not infinite, and their productivity growth is in itself hard to accelerate. Therefore, there is a limit on their contribution to productivity growth.

The consumption-oriented service sectors and logistics sectors are labor-intensive and hard to raise productivity. The larger these sectors' share of GDP, the slower the total productivity growth.

In conclusion, productivity growth and economic growth falls while service as a share of GDP increases. In 2014, China's service sector has surpassed manufacturing as a share of GDP, and this trend is certain to continue. Therefore, the productivity growth dividend will gradually vanish.

(iv) The reform dividend shrinks

The Chinese economy has achieved a high degree of commercialization and marketization, even approaching the level of mature market economies. However, the government still looms large in investment, financing and other factor markets, severely distorting the economic system. From an economic perspective, it distorts market signals, separates economic development from objective conditions such as resource and environment, and results in structural distortion. From a social perspective, it distorts social values, encourages corruption, and exacerbates discontent and unrest. Undoubtedly, productivity would be unleashed and innovation encouraged by reforming the institutions that constrain healthy economic development. Economic reform must be accelerated in order to maintain a healthy and steady economic growth and social stability.

It is widely acknowledged that China's high economic growth of more than three decades could be attributed to the Reform and Opening Up of 1978. The reforms before 2010 were evidently inclusive. Although benefits of the reforms were spread unevenly and income inequality soared, almost everyone benefited from them and nobody incurred losses, which is a Pareto optimal state. However, more deepening reforms in the future are bound to touch vested interests, whose holders tend to be powerful people. Therefore, reform will be more challenging, and the reform dividend of economic growth will shrink a great deal.

a. Reform reduces the incentive of local governments to blindly pursue sheer GDP growth

The fourth plenary session of the 18th CPC Central Committee decided to "comprehensively advance the rule of law". However, China still has a very long way to go towards a society with authentic rule of law. From an economic perspective, the government has an overly strong hand in economic development, straining its resources for other social functions. As a result, the government is overly active in driving economic growth and insufficiently active in social management. It constantly oversteps its bounds in the economy, where there is ample opportunity for rent-seeking and rent-creating. Meanwhile, it is struggling to fulfil its functions in social management, where rent-seeking opportunities are rare. This phenomenon is manifest in governments at all levels.

The government tends to overstep its bounds in the economy. It is an overly active economic agent in investment and construction. It also uses administrative measures to extensively intervene in the market access, operation mode, and project approval of businesses. Such overstepping persists eventhough the current government decided to transform government functions, abolished many approval requirements, and made it easier to for business startups to get regisreied. First, the government frequently replaces the market in the allocation of resources. It intervenes in the operation of the economy through a vast array of state-owned enterprises (SOE). It also wields its administrative powers to vet business projects. For example, the government is directly involved in land allocation and approval of the establishment of large businesses. It also directly participates in some of the projects. Second, the government still extensively meddles in the operation of SOEs. The government in effect runs SOEs through personnel appointments and administrative interventions, taking the responsibility for business operations that should be reserved for businesses themselves. Third, the government, in its role as supervisor or partner, directly intervenes in the management and operations of associations, communities, and urban and rural autonomous organizations, in effect reducing them to a subordinate of the government or even a conduit of rent-seeking and rent-creating. These behaviors are closely related to performance evaluations that local governments are regularly subject to, and also related to rent-seeking and corruption. The government fails to do what the law mandates it to do, and frequently oversteps into what the law does not mandate it to do. As a result, local governments exhausted their financial capacity and incurred dangerous level of debt in pursuit of economic growth targets. Land is overdeveloped as a source of government finance and an attraction of investment. Prevalent large projects result in a severe problem of excess capacity. Real estate is overheated, creating many "empty cities" and "ghost cities". The high economic growth of the past 30 years came at a price for future generations, paving the way for a potential financial crisis. There are also consequences for social development. Money is put above everything else. The government suffers from officials' corruption and decreasing credibility. Social values are severely distorted. Corrupt officials are negligent where there is no chance of rent-seeking, and overzealous where there is significant chance.

Since the 18th CPC National Congress, the central government adopted a strategy of "comprehensively deepening reforms" and rolled out a series of deepening reforms. It weakened local governments' growth targets, and reduced local governments' pressure to pursue economic growth. Reforms of government functions have streamlined government and delegated authorities. These, along with the campaign against corruption, has reduced the incerrtive of local governments to drive economic growth, curbing the unstable growth based on the exhaustion of financial abilities. As long as reform and anti-corruption becomes the norm, China's economy will grow more normally and fill the gap of public finance in the future.

Meanwhile, the government is struggling to fulfil its functions in some non-economic areas, especially public services and environment protection. It is conspicuously absent in many public services. For example, in the past 30 years of high growth, the government has neglected the management of ecology and the environment. Some local governments, in the pursuit of economic gains, even collaborated with polluting businesses to circumvent law enforcement and supervision from national environment authorities. They are obsessed with resource exploitation and production, but negligent of ecosystem recovery and environment protection. As a result, China's natural environment has exhausted and even collapsed in some regions, which means future economic development must compensate for the environmental loss at the same time. This is one of the main reasons why China's growth is slowing. What's more, local governments are overly keen on building "new cities" and other real estate projects to increase government revenue. On the other hand, they frequently neglect the need to build primary education and public health facilities. Take Yanjiao, a "development zone" east of Beijing. There the municipality of Langfang built a provincial-level economic development zone. It is now a "sleeper city" with 600,000 people.

The population is very young, with a majority born after the 1980s. There is large demand for kindergartens, elementary and middle schools. However, the government is obsessively focused on real estate development, neglecting the need for education. Class size at public schools is a whopping 90. Even so, only well-connected families are able to send their children in. Some low-income young families bought houses and moved to Yanjiao, only to find their children unable to go to school or have to enroll in unaffordable private schools.

With the implementation of rule of law and growing public awareness, the government's economic overstepping and social neglect is bound to be corrected. In the 2015 Report on the Work of the Government, Premier Li Keqiang pointed out that the government has powers but must not use them arbitrarily. This means that governments will stop blindly pursuing sheer GDP growth, bringing economic growth back to the natural level.

b. Reforms of macroeconomic regulations will reduce the distortion of market information and turn the economy into "normal" growth levels

The grave mistakes in macroeconomic regulations in the past decade have severely distorted market signals. Microeconomic agents, like local governments and businesses, has overreacted to these distorted signals and driven an abnormal growth of the economy. As a result, excess capacity has become a serious problem, industrial organization and structure has worsened, and malign competition ensued. Take the steel industry as an example. In 2001-10, the government imposed strict restrictions on the steel industry. The rationale was that China's demand of steel would be 300 million tons by 2010, but annual production had already reached 222 million tons and capacity neared 300 million tons by 2003. Moreover, more steel projects were being built at that time. Figuring in these projects, the total potential production capacity would exceed 400 million tons. Therefore, the government in 2003 rolled out the strictest ever restrictions on steel investments. It halted approvals of the establishment of large steel businesses, and froze credit flows to those businesses. However, after 2003, rising domestic and foreign aggregate demand pushed up the demand of steel. Its price soared as a result. Building small-scale steel factories became one of the most rewarding investment options, so much so that investment costs could be recouped within a year. Stimulated by those distorted signals, local governments collaborated with investors to circumvent restrictions on large steel businesses by establishing a myriad of small steel corporations. The result was that advanced technologies, which only large businesses possessed, were limited. But various small steel factories had sprouted everywhere. Consequently, the steel industry was very fragmented, with dismal technology structure and high resource consumption and pollution. In 2010, China's actual demand for steel reached 600 million tons, but production capacity reached 1 billion tons, only 400 million of which was legally approved by the central government. This created both the excess capacity seen today and a lot of technically illegal businesses. And the steel industry is just a tip of the iceberg. Similar problems occurred in cement, aluminum, electricity, coal and other industries. Excessive regulative power based on incorrect projections has also created a lot of corrupt officials. The so-called "macroeconomic regulation" of the steel and heavy industries turned out to be completely failed micromanagement. Eventually, under the pressure of energy consumption and natural environment, China had to implement the world's strictest measures to phase out and replace backward capacities. The country's steel production capacity was projected to reach 1.1-1.2 billion tons in 2014. Those excess capacity led to malignant cut-throat competition, incurring losses for most steel businesses.

We can see that China's problem of excess capacities is largely the result of market overreaction to the government's distortion of market signals. It not only spurred anti-market excessive growth, but also led to excess capacity and a huge waste of resources and capital. Furthermore, Chinese businesses mainly rely on bank credit as their source of financing. Overcapacity led to low efficiency or even losses, incurring great risk on the financial sector. It is evident that the new round of deepening reforms since 2014 would be more and more difficult. Its potential for facilitating economic development would also be significantly lower than the first round of reform, which simply aimed at unleashing and developing productivity.

(v) The vanishing environment dividend becomes a hard constraint on growth

In the early time of Reform and Opening Up, when China's industrialization was just started, the environment could endure a relatively large amount of pollution, misleading people to believe that the environment had an infinite absorption capacity. China passed an environmental protection law as early as 1989. But as of 2014, businesses could still pollute free of charge if their pollution level was below a certain threshold; only when inspectors caught above-level pollution did the businesses pay a fee. Domestic producers and consumers have been freely using the environment as a public resource to emit all kinds of waste. As a result, prices do not figure in environmental costs. Resource exploitation has also put a lot of strain on the ecosystem. Most miners paid no effort towards ecological recovery, meaning that price levels also do not include ecological damages. The past 30 years of high economic growth is achieved at the price of ecological and environmental exhaustion. China's current ecological damage and environmental pollution has far crossed the red line of what the environment can bear. The environment dividend has completely vanished. The ecosystem and the environment will certainly collapse if the country continues to adopt the previous approach to ecosystem and waste disposal. The environment has become a hard constraint on economic growth. Future economic growth must at the same time compensate for the losses in ecosystems and environment, greatly raising the environmental cost of growth. As a result, the country's growth potential is reduced.

(vi) The resource dividend vanishes, constraining economic growth

We used to think China as a country with vast territory and abundant resources. But people have realized since the start of industrialization that the country's *per capita* resource level is very low. From land and water to minerals, China's per capita resource is far from abundant. More than three decades of industrialization has depleted most of the country's high quality mineral resources. Water shortages have become more severe by the day. Energy and resource costs have crept up. Land resources have declined to the extent that food security is threatened. By 2020, China would import 70% of its oil and iron ore consumption, and more than 90% of copper and rubber. The resource dividend of economic growth has vanished. Take the example of iron ore. China's iron ore reserve and its grade is both low. Its mining relies mainly on low labor costs and extensive environmental damages. China is mining iron ore the iron content of which is as low as 20% or maybe even lower, while in Australia iron ore with lessthan 45% iron content is considered of poor quality. Although oil and commodity prices have slumped since 2013, resource prices are certain to rebound due to the rise of India and other emerging economies and the recovery of world economy. The resource cost of China's economic growth will continue to rise. The vanishing of resource dividend makes it hard to sustain high economic growth that relies on cheap resources, especially of land, coal and water.

(vii) The vanishing urbanization dividend slows down economic growth

The Chinese government briefly tried a "deurbanizing" way of industrialization in the 1980-90s. It attempted to achieve industrialization by developing rural enterprises, saying that farmers should "leave their home but not the rural area, enter the factories but not the cities". The deurbanizing approach spread industries across the vast countryside. It could not achieve economies of scale, and nor could it solve the pollution problem that came with industrial development. By the end of 1990s, the country could no longer sustain this approach that counters the basic rules of economic development. Furthermore, after the 1997 Asian crisis, the export-driven Chinese economy encountered some difficulties. Falling international demand made it hard to sustain the previous development model where rural enterprises export extensively. Excessive inventory ensued, bankrupting a lot of rural enterprises. In order to seek new driving forces of growth, China finally began to conform to basic economic rules since the tenth five-year plan. The government combined industrialization with urbanization, allowing the rural population to migrate into cities in order to enlarge domestic demand. Then, China's industries began to consolidate in and around cities. Urbanization became an important part of economic development. Therefore, it was not until 2000 that the government began to saw urbanization as one of its main task.

China's urbanization has been accelerating since 2000. Its cities added 17.20 million people per year during 1996-2000, with urbanization rate rising by 1.15% per year. The figures rose to 20.16 million and 1.35%, respectively, during 2001-05, and to 21.53 million and 1.39% during 2006-10. However, with urbanization rising and the existing urban population growing, the annual urban population growth has slowed to 18.05 million in 2014, and urbanization rate grew by 1.04% annually, slower than the 1.15% of 1996-2000.

Although China's urbanization rate will continue to rise, the growth rate is gradually falling. Note that urban productivity, per capita income and consumption are all 3 times that of rural areas. Therefore, rising urbanization engenders rising economic rates. A growing urbanization rate translates into a dividend for economic growth. Conversely, slowing growth of urbanization means that the urbanization dividend is shrinking, and economic growth slowing.

Table 3 Changes in China's urbanization rate, 1996-2014

	Annual growth in urban population (million)	Annual urbanization growth rate (%)
1996-2000	17.20	1.15
2001-2005	20.16	1.35
2006-2010	21.53	1.39
2011	21.01	1.32
2012	21.03	1.30
2013	19.29	1.16
2014	18.05	1.04

Source: *China Statistical Yearbook 2014. Data for 2014 is also compiled from the Statistical Communiqué on the 2014 National Economic and Social Development.*

(viii) The vanishing net export dividend drags down economic growth

Net export dividend is defined as the contribution to economic growth of net export in goods and services. Since the late 1970s, the contribution of net export to economic growth has been large, becoming an important driving force of growth. China's net export has been growing rapidly, especially in the period between China's entry into WTO in 2001 and the financial crisis in 2008. However, since the 2008 crisis spread globally, China's net export growth has slowed or even reverse. Table 4 shows that net export in goods and services declined during 2011-13. Its pushing effect on economic growth vanished, meaning the net export dividend also vanished. In 2014, net export of goods and services growth by 82.04 billion yuan, but that does not mean net export will begin a new cycle of growth. There are two main reasons for the increase in net export in 2014. First, import growth slowed along with the domestic economy. Imports of goods grew by only 0.4% that year. Secondly, prices of China's main imports, including oil and mineral resources, fell precipitously. Import growth measured by value was significantly lower than measured by volume. This is an exception, not the norm in the future. Note that although the year 2014 was exceptional in that way, the contribution of net export to GDP was still merely 0.73%.

Table 4 The contribution of net export to China's GDP

Year	Contribution (%)	Year	Contribution (%)
1990	50.4	2011	-4.2
1995	0.3	2012	-2.1
2000	12.5	2013	-4.4
2005	22.2	2014	0.73
2010	4.0		

Source: *China Statistical Yearbook 2014. Data for 2014 is also compiled from the Statistical Communiqué on the 2014 National Economic and Social Development.*

In rich countries, economic recovery is a long-term process. Rising costs of manufacturing means that the competitiveness of Chinese products will fall. Also,

China is adjusting its balance of payment in reaction to its overly large foreign currency reserves. All these factors mean that the net export dividend is certain to vanish, and its contribution to GDP growth also gradually vanishes.

The above analysis show that, as China's economic development enters a period of stage transition and institutional change, the eight growth dividends either shrink or vanish. Slower economic growth becomes inevitable.

Transition of development stages is dictated by the objective rules of industrialization and development, and is not subject to human will. Deepening reform of the distorted economic system is necessary in order to guarantee sustainable and steady socioeconomic development. Therefore, the "new normal" of China's economy would be development under painful structural changes of later-stage industrialization. Cut-throat competition and survival of the fittest will continue in traditional sectors. Meanwhile, economic development must be accompanied by reforms centered on correcting economic distortions, transforming government functions and relaxing government control. The abnormal, impulsive and government-driven growth will weaken. And future development must compensate for the past losses and gaps in public finance, resources, ecosystems and the environment, further rising the social cost of future economic development. The population dividend will irreversibly vanish, raising the microeconomic business cost of economic growth and lowering China's international competitiveness. The shrinking or even vanishing of the net export dividend will significantly weaken the external driving force of economic growth. The fall in TFP growth directly turns down the internal growth engine. A combination of these factors means that future economic growth is bound to slow down. This is the core economic connotation of the "new normal" of the Chinese economy. We cannot tell what exactly this "new normal" will look like and how long it will last. The "new normal" concept that Xi Jinping described at APEC conference, the 2014 Central Economic Working Conference, and the 2015 Report on the Work of the Government are mainly some expectations and policy orientations of China's political leadership. They also represent a policy thinking that aims at combating the difficulties prought along by the "new normal".

Chapter 4

Distinguishing Between Normality, Abnormality and the New Normal

In the debate about the new normal of China's economy, many Chinese scholars have failed to distinguish between normality, abnormality and the new normal of the market economy. They tend to regard the "market economy normal" as China's economic new normal.

I. Normality

Normality is the state of being usual or typical. Economic normality is the natural or normal stage of economic development. As discussed above, each country has its unique situation, so the term "normality" is relative to the conditions of the particular object in discussion. There are fundamental differences between the normality of a market economy and that of a planned economy. Under the conditions of a market economy, supply tends to exceed demand, and the normality usually consists of excess capacity. The United States is generally considered as the economy with the greatest market freedom. Therefore, the operating principles and macroeconomic conditions of the American economy can be regarded as the normality of a market economy. America's capacity utilization rate, which is a good indicator of market competitiveness, stands at an average of only 78.7% in the manufacturing sector from 1972 to 2013. If we take this 40-year average as America's normality, we can infer that the market normality entails a 22% excess manufacturing capacity. This is because competition is only possible with an appropriate amount of excess capacity, which in turn fosters technological innovation in enterprises. It is precisely the cut-throat competition in domestic and international markets that made America the most technologically advanced and innovative country in the world.

Table 5 Capacity Utilization Rate of U.S., 1972-2013 (%)

Capacity Utilization Rate	1972-2013	1988-89	1990-91	1994-95	2009	Jan 2013	Dec 2013	Jan 2014	Sep 2014
Average	80.1	85.2	78.8	85	66.9	77.7	78.9	78.5	80.1
Manufacturing	78.7	85.6	77.3	84.6	64	76.2	76.7	76	77.3
Mining	87.4	86.3	83.9	88.6	78.3	87.3	90.3	89.2	
Public Utility	86	92.9	84.3	93.3	78.6	76.9	80.1	83.3	
Oil	86.3	87.7	84.4	89.7	76.4	86.2	88.3	87.3	
Primary Goods	80.9	86.5	78	87.9	64.4	75.9	77.6	77.8	
Finished Goods	77.1	83.4	77.3	80.6	66.8	76	76	75.2	

Source: *blog.163.com before Jan 2014, and fx678.com for Sep 2014.*

The market economy has short-term and technical supply shortages as well. For example, when a new and popular product goes to market, it takes time to build its manufacturing capacity, which results in a short-term situation where demand exceeds supply and creates a shortage. But this situation will not last long. The tendency of capital to pursue profit will lead capital to flow into these newfound sectors, resulting in a glut. Hunger marketing from monopolistic firms can also lead to short-term shortages of popular products. But as technology spread quickly nowadays, competitors will use imitation to force the monopolies to end their hunger marketing.

It remains to be researched regarding just how high China's capacity utilization rate is and whether the economy is at the market normality. Take steel again as an example. According to the National Statistical Bureau, China's steel production capacity was 990 million tons in 2013, and actual steel production was 779 million tons, which means that China's steel capacity utilization rate in 2013 was also 78.7%, exactly the same as in the United States in 1972-2013. China's steel should be at market normality instead of suffering from severe excess[1]. It seems that the so-called "excess capacity" is a false proposition, at least not an important problem, that is resulted from microeconomic interventions. As long as the government does not overly interfere and distort the market, the firms will automatically react to competition in the market normality. For instance, some heavy industries have a capacity utilization rate of below 70%. That is because local governments, in their blind pursuit of economic growth numbers, excessively woo outside investments and engage in repetitive production, which also caters to some firms' desire to seize as much land as possible.

II. Abnormality

According to basic economic theories, resource allocation in economic development should be decided by market actors through competition and supply and demand. That is to say, the market plays a decisive role in allocating resources. The "shortages" where demand exceeds supply should not last long. With free competition and the price mechanism, both shortages and the

---

1   However, when we consider the market competitiveness and profit level of China's steel industry in 2013, we can infer that China's steel capacity utilization rate cannot possibly be 78.7%. Note that rich countries such as America and Japan usually also have a utilization rate of below 80%, but these countries never experienced cut-throat competition and massive losses like China's steel industry did. One possibility is that the steel capacity figures from China's National Statistical Bureau are gravely wrong, and the actual steel capacity might be far higher than the official statistics, which means that the utilization rate should be well below 78.7%. This is because of the central government's periodical evaluations of local energy and emission levels. The steel industry is one of the main sources of SO_2 emission, and China's current steel furnaces are mostly not desulfurated. Cooking the books on steel capacity can help local governments to fulfil sulfur emission targets. This assumption is supported by the steel industry: the industry's estimate of the utilization rate is around 72%.

equilibrium are abnormalities. China's economy before 1996 was at such an abnormality. Then, the demand of almost all of China's products exceeds supply. According to the national bureau of statistics, China's domestic products have all experienced shortage or equilibrium except palm oil. The year 1996 was the turning point of China's economy from abnormality towards market normality. China's market abnormality before 1996 has led to high-speed economic growth. In 2001, China has emerged from the 1997 Asian crisis and entered a new stage of rapid development. From then until 2008, the economy again experienced supply shortages and price rises, turning into economic abnormality again. Why did this happen? The main reason is that China's macroeconomic policymakers have always aimed at an equilibrium between demand and supply. But as we analyzed above, the equilibrium is actually a case of market abnormality. This has been the main dilemma facing China's macroeconomic policy: the country wants to adopt market economy, but meanwhile tries to use central planning to keep the aforementioned abnormalities. It is precisely this distorted and self-contradictory logic that impeded China's macroeconomic regulations.Regulators made futile attempts to keep the economy running under market abnormality, especially in 2003-12 when macroeconomic regulations relied mainly on central planning. The government intervened too much in the economy, the reforms backtracked, the state advanced but the private sector retreated in many industries. The objectives of central and local governments were increasingly in conflict. On the one hand, in order to control prices, the central government mistakenly judged the market situation and placed arbitrary restrictions on rational investments and restrained the growth of effective demand, worsening industry structure and organization. On the other hand, in order to boost growth figures, local governments led expansions in investment, increasing market demand and stimulated the development of backward capacities. As a result, market demand increased a great deal. The government responded to the 2008 financial crisis with administrative forces again, launching a 4 trillion-yuan stimulus package instead of reforming the economy and let it adjust according to market forces. This phenomenon lasted as late as 2012. It can be said that the Chinese economy during this period is at a market economy "abnormality".

III. Transformation between Normality, Abnormality and the New Normal

It goes without saying that free competition and excess supply is the economic normality under a market economy. According to Marxist economic theories, capitalist market economies have cyclical economic crises, which is also a normality of the capitalist economy. However, after the onset of an economic crisis, the government intervenes in the economy and push it into an "abnormality". If the intervention and the resulting economic changes are short-lived and do not fundamentally change the rules, mechanisms, structure and mode of the economy, then the economy will return to normal after a brief period of abnormality. On the contrary, if government interventions fundamentally change the economy, its development will enter a stage of "new normal". The United States changed its financial rules, mechanism and structure after the 2008 financial crisis, strengthened government regulation, and is undergoing constant changes in the market structure, so the American economy can be said to have entered a "new normal".

China is still not a mature market economy. It is still undergoing a transition towards one. Its original economic system is one of central planning. According to JánosKornai, a renowned Hungarian economist, the normality of a planned economy is shortages. That is to say, shortage economy is the "normality of planned economies" and the "abnormality of market economies". Therefore, when we describe the stages of economic development with the terms "normality" and "abnormality", we have to specify the context. Considering in this sense President Xi Jinping's speech in Henan and at the APEC conference in Beijing, the term "new normal" does not only refer to a stage of economic development. It also means that the status of China's socioeconomic development is transforming from the "old normal" of the 30 years since China's opening up, when the economy was at the preliminary stages of industrialization with distorted profit and industry structures and disharmony between human and nature, towards a new normal of "new development stage" where the economy relies more on market rules and fits more into the objective demands of later-stage industrialization with more reasonable benefit allocation and more harmony between human and nature.

This new development stage means that economic growth has slowed down from the previous rate of around 10% to around 7%. Especially, the traditional manufacturing sectors will end its overheated growth of more than 20% and turn into low-to-middle speed of growth. Competition will thrive, and prices and utility will fall. The window is closing for economic growth to be driven by simply increasing investments and expanding capacity. Only by continuous innovation can the economy keep growing. And innovation needs the accumulation of knowledge and human capital. It also needs the reconstruction of institutions and environment that is beneficial to innovation. It needs to be able to shoulder the risk of failure, and needs time for the innovations to spread and materialize. This means that those enterprises and regions that are unwilling or unable to innovate will face increasing economic pressure.

In the aspect of institutions, the hard constraints of ecological and environmental regulations mean that the days are gone when the economy can freely grow at the expense of increasing emissions and sacrifices to the ecosystem. Demographic changes mean that the growth of labor supply is slowing down, and the economy can no longer grow with the help of unlimited supply of cheap labor and the sacrifice of migrant workers' rights. Firms' production costs are growing, and profit margins are becoming thinner.

Slowing growth of demand, rising costs and falling competitiveness means that the economy can no longer grow by importing technology and equipment to quickly build capacity and replicate mature industries and expand manufacturing exports at low costs.

Because the primary distribution of income is biased towards businesses and governments, income inequality is high and there is a severe imbalance between consumption and accumulation. The economy can no longer grow by government borrowing and investment expansion which boosts domestic demand of investment.

These phenomena reflect profound changes in China's economic environments, and the changes might be irreversible. This means that China's economic development must adapt to these changes. If we consider the changes in a market economy context, we can define it as a transformation from abnormality to normality – the Chinese economy has entered the market economy normal. To use the terminology with Chinese characteristics, we can also define it as a transformation from the "old normal" with Chinese characteristics towards a "new normal".

Chapter 5

Policy Measures in the Face of New Normal

In summary of the analysis above, we believe that the reason why China's economy enters the new normal is that the transformation of development stages causes the eight growth dividends to shrink or vanish. In order to react to the difficulties of the new normal, the economy must adapt to the demands of stage transformation and utilize the remaining growth dividends that still have potential, and create new growth dividends to replace the previously vanishing ones. Then the economy would be able to growth at a fast and steady pace, and create material foundation and institutional conditions for solving the myriad of socioeconomic problems that arise with development. In response to the new normal, China should comprehensively implement the following seven strategies: comprehensive reform strategy, innovation-driven development strategy, human resource nurturing strategy, circular economy strategy, substantial urbanization strategy, manufacturing and emerging industries upgrading strategy, and trade in services improvement strategy.

I. The comprehensive reform strategy to cope with shrinking reform dividend

In order to cope with the shrinking reform dividend, China should explore the potential for institutional reform, lower the social cost of transaction, and improve commercial freedom and economic efficiency. Reform is a huge, complicated and systematic social project, involving the material and political interest of all members of society. The main methodology of the post-1978 reforms is the theory of practice: practice is the sole criterion for testing truth, and efficiency should be put above all else. Deng Xiaoping's famous "cat quote" is a growth theory that prioritizes efficiency and the development of productive forces. Deng's policy of "letting some people get rich first" has stimulated the people's passion for innovation and creation. The country sustained more than 30 years of high-speed growth with the help of the eight growth dividends. The economic pie has grown larger, and everyone benefited from the reforms. However, a major transformation is needed between the reform path of "letting some people get rich first" and the ultimate goal of "common prosperity". The country must fill the widening gap between the haves and the haves-not. Because of the Matthew effect of the market economy, inequality is rising between the firstly rich people and the masses, which poses a growing threat to social stability and justice. Especially, some of the upper class got rich not through hard work and intelligence, but through rent seeking and corruption. They do not number many, but have contaminated and even divided the civil society, pushed up the transaction costs, lowered social efficiency, and deprived the rest of the population of the opportunities to get rich. China needs a second round of reform to fill the gap of inequality and engineer a smooth transition towards common prosperity.

The essence of reform is to lower the social transaction cost through institutional innovation. It stimulates members of society to engage in innovation and increase the efficiency of social operation and innovation, and provide equal development opportunities for all citizens. This would facilitate the development of production forces, increase social wealth, and increase the level of human development and freedom.

The third plenary session of the 18th Central Committee of CPC made the decision to comprehensively deepen reforms. Some of the reforms have already been announced, and many more are still in the making. We believe that reform in the following aspects is very important in order to cope with the new normal and maintain economic growth.

(i) Accelerating reforms that aim at lowering transaction costs

The most important function of institutions is to lower the transaction costs in a society. If a set of institutions keep increasing these costs, the fluidity of social resources will weaken, and the institutions will collapse from within. The biggest problem of China's socialist market economy in the past 20 years was the growing transaction costs and the increasing difficulty of resource flow. On the one hand, the government played an outsized role in the control of resources. Unnecessary approval processes and rampant corruption severely stymied the free flow and optimal combination of resources. On the other hand, the collusion of power and business created a lot of monopolistic interest groups that controls resource allocation, effectively forming economic fiefdoms that increased business transaction costs and severely hampered economic development and distributional justice. Therefore, China should accelerate reforms that aim at lowering transaction costs.

Since the 18th CPC Congress, the State Council has led the reform of government functions and cancelled a lot of administrative approval processes, releasing energy for the free flow of social resources. The corresponding anti-corruption campaign has effectively deterred officials from rent seeking, also lowering transaction costs to some degree. However, the salary income of government officials is still too low compared with their responsibilities and work. The anti-corruption campaign has thus caused some officials to be slack in work. Without adequate reform of government functions, the slack will also cause transaction costs to rise. Two things must be done to tackle this problem. First, reform of government functions and delegation should be accelerated, and the number of public officials reduced. Second, it is time to substantially increase the formal pay and welfare of public officials in order to create effective incentives.

As for the problem of oligarchical control that impedes the free flow of resources, reforms should deepen in the aspects of property rights and state-owned asset management. The recruitment of management professionals for state-owned assets should be public in order to break insider control. For privately-owned monopolies, anti-monopoly legislations and regulations should be introduced.

The rule of law should also be truly implemented. The law is a set of transparent and formal rules with explicit procedures that the whole society should abide by. when the government governs by law, transaction costs and risks would be lowered. The more stable and comprehensive the laws, the lower the transaction costs.

(ii) Deepening reforms that stimulates mass innovation

Innovation is the soul of human development. Good institutions can facilitate mass innovation, and bad institutions impede it. The motivations behind innovations are complex: there are economic objectives, curiosity, and self-consciousness and self-achievement objectives. In a market economy, the primary objective of innovation is to acquire more disposable wealth. Therefore, institutions must enable innovators to achieve that goal through innovation. It should also help facilitate unimpeded spread of innovation outcomes in order to benefit the whole society. The following principles should be adhered to in the process of institutional design.

(1)   Realizing the value of innovators' labor. Innovators have to accumulate human capital and invest a lot of labor time. Many innovative researchers work for far more than the legally stipulated 8 hours a day and without holidays. The current payment system does not adequately compensate for their highly intelligent work. This system should be revamped to reverse the mistake of the existing system that put little value in researchers' work.

(2)   Establish and improve the sharing of innovation outcome. China's present

market and evaluation for innovation outcomes is deeply flawed, and innovators often find it hard to get adequate returns, which stymies their passion to innovate.

(3)   Accelerate the reform of investment and financing of small and middle businesses. These businesses are not only the main creator of jobs but also the most active innovators. Small businesses in the tech sector, in particular, are the foundation of massive amount of original innovation. These businesses now face severe constraints in the access and cost of financing. Angel investment is still very rudimentary, and venture capital lags far behind the demand of small businesses. Reforms should be deepened regarding the investment and financing of small and middle businesses. The financial system should be innovated. For example, tax incentives could be given to encourage the establishment of angel funds and startup funds. The state could also establish a specialized fund to support small tech businesses and help them shoulder the risks that come with innovation.

(iii) Reforms that increase human development and freedom and facilitate social harmony

Human development and freedom is the foundation of social harmony and the ultimate goal of society. Since the start of the 21st century, China has made significant progress in social management. The free movement of people has improved a great deal. Population flows spread knowledge, change minds, and create urges to innovate. Reforms in this aspect should focus on increasing the freedom to choose where to live, to receive education, to choose jobs and lifestyle. The state should accelerate reforms of the household registration system, social security, and talent management, in order to make these systems uniform across the country.

It is without doubt that, contrary to the first round of reform starting in 1978, this new, second round of reform is a re-reform on the basis of the previous, inclusive reform. It is bound to touch the vested interests of some beneficiaries of the last round of reform, and encounter greater resistance.

II. The innovation-driven development strategy to cope with shrinking productivity dividend

Innovation is an instinct that is intrinsic in the human mind. With the right external conditions, this instinct will be activated, and innovation becomes the main driving force of economic and social activities. The innovation-driven development strategy requires institutional and managerial reform to activate the innovation instinct, accelerate technological and commercial innovation, and achieve economic development on the basis of innovation-driven development.

There are different understandings of innovation-driven development. Some people believe that it merely means economic growth driven by technological innovation. In fact, technological innovation is the result and materialization of innovation *per se* in the production process, but not the driving force of innovation. Only by creating incentives and mechanism that is conducive for all members of society to innovate, can the economy develop a satisfactory innovation environment. Innovation, including in management, technology and business model, would then become the primary driving force of social development.

(i) Accelerate institutional innovation and improve innovation mechanism

The main task of institutional innovation is to improve innovation mechanism and create satisfactory environment for managerial, technological and commercial innovation. It increases the incentive and enthusiasm of the innovators. This is the highest level of innovation. Only when there is progress in institutional innovation can there be innovation-driven development. Deepening reforms are needed for institutional innovation. The third plenary session of the 18th Central Committee of CPC has made comprehensive arrangements of reforms of the economic system. In order to implement the innovation-driven development strategy, the reforms should emphasize incentives for innovators and lighten the load of enterprises (especially small and middle businesses that are innovative). In the aspects of taxes, investment and financing, the state should give proper incentives to stimulate the enthusiasm for R&D and other investment in innovation. Mechanisms should also be established that benefits talent and encourages the populace to engage in innovation.

Since 1995, China has implemented a series of reform measures to create effective incentives through institutional innovation. The core of these reforms is the profit incentive of innovators. In March 2014, the State Council issued *Some Opinions on Improving and Strengthening the Management of Scientific Research Projects and Funding*. This document proposed some new regulations regarding the use of scientific research funding from the public coffers, and has important meaning for reforms on the subject. Article 27 of the *Opinions* states that institutions and policies should be improved regarding the stimulation of innovation. These include:improving income distribution of scientific researchers, establish a distribution and incentive mechanism that is closely linked with job responsibilities and performance and contribution; improving the flow of scientific talent, encouraging the two-way exchange between research institutions, universities and businesses; accelerating the reform of the management of use, handling and profits of research outcomes, improving such policies that facilitate the materialization of research; strengthen the use and protection of intellectual property rights; implement tax policies that encourage technological innovation; accelerate the reform of scientific evaluation and awarding, setting assessment standards that has a clear aim and place equal importance on incentive and restraint; fully utilize the creativity of project undertakers and researchers. But the Opinions only outlined some principles and directions, which needs further details to implement.

Presently, there is a serious problem in the innovation incentives of researchers in state-owned research institutions and universities. That is, how to strengthen the status of these researchers on the chain of profit distribution. For example, current regulations forbid high-level officials in research institutions and universities to take part-time positions in businesses or start their own businesses. These regulations severed the ties between these officials and businesses. The researchers are unable to receive their deserved benefits from their contribution of innovative services to businesses and the society. The increasingly tight budget constraint means that the real income of many researchers are actually falling, creating a disincentive and severely hampers the enthusiasm of researchers to engage in innovative work. This phenomenon needs close attention.

(ii) Facilitate innovation in management

Management innovation is the deepening of the practical aspects of institutional innovation. The focus of management innovation is the management of factor allocation, factors circulation, benefit incentives, and the spread of innovation outcomes.

The innovation on the management of optimal resource allocation should be done in two parts. First, market mechanism should be enhanced. In the areas where the market is relatively mature, the government should be determined to delegate its powers and reduce intervention, letting the market play its fundamental role in resource allocation. The state should increase the autonomous power of research institutions and universities to allocate and use resources related to innovation. Second, in the areas with little or immature market competition, the government should increase its support for innovation, lower its risks, and help innovators in the application and spread of innovation outcomes.

The innovation of factors circulation management requires strict distinction between public officials and the leading officials in research institutions and universities. The government should not manage and regulate high-level university officials in the same way as public officials in government. The state should encourage but not restrict scientific researchers to take part-time positions in businesses, research institutions and universities. The facilitation of the flow of the most innovative people can increase the flow and spread of knowledge and technology, and is beneficial to the spread of innovation outcomes.

(iii) Comprehensively pushing technological innovation

The meaning of technological innovation is: to accumulate and use new knowledge and new technologies to create value efficiently; increasing reliance of the economy on the optimal combination of resources; develop new technology, means of production, recyclable resources, new products and new industries; adopt green and clean production methods, use precise information management, improve the efficiency of resource use, and achieve endogenous and sustainable economic growth.

To improve technological innovation, the emphasis should be put on the following two directions. First, policymakers should fully utilize market competition and stimulate businesses to increase their competitiveness through innovation. Second, the government should create institutional environments that are beneficial to businesses' technological innovation, research institutions' R&D on new knowledge and technology, and universities' cultivation of innovative talent. The government should also facilitate intermediate agencies to materialize and spread. It should also establish the main direction and expected breakthroughs in vital strategical sectors by increasing investments and grasp key technologies and lead the market in technological innovation.

(1) Facilitating the reform and reorganization of the national technological innovation system. Technological innovation is a complicated systematic project which goes on continuously and dynamically. It is supported by the national innovation system, which consists of innovative enterprises, research and development institutions, and social scientific intermediary organizations. Its task is to facilitate the effective division and combination of these players. They have their own positions and functions on the chain of technological innovation. In the process of facilitating innovation-driven development, they must combine effectively and cooperate closely in information dissemination, development and application of knowledge and technology, talent flow, and allocation of innovative resources. Therefore, an important aspect of deepening economic reform is the reform and optimization of the national technological innovation system.

(2) In some vital sectors with strong externalities, such as the environment,

public health, social security, national defense, frontline technology, national innovation plans should be continuously implemented. The government should fully utilize market mechanism and increase investment at the same time, in order to provide strong scientific reserve and technological support for completing the process of building a moderately prosperous society.

(3)   The deepening of reforms should replace the project approval processes with market access vetting that emphasize on environmental standards in all competitive fields. The government should encourage and strengthen market competition and use the invisible hand to facilitate technological innovation from businesses.

(iv) Facilitate innovation of business models

The innovation of business models is the foundation of the wide spread and application of innovation outcomes. Its key is to acquire more competitiveness by providing clients with new goods and service models, minimizing transaction costs and maximizing profits while acquiring the ability of sustainable development. Especially for the new products that are based on the internet economy and rely on digitization, the innovation of business models determines whether innovation outcomes can translate into competitive advantage of the businesses. The electrical car is a typical example of the importance of business model innovation. It represents the trend of future development of the automobile industry, but it has not yet been popularized due to a lack of battery charging networks and other problems regarding business model.

Jack Ma has created a miracle in the age of the internet, pushing China to the global front of e-commerce. The success of his e-commerce empire is not because he created some unprecedented technology, but because he fully utilized the available information technology and created a new business model. In the field of sales and marketing, the industry has developed from street vendors to shopping malls, to supermarkets, and to Mr. Ma's e-commerce model. The sales of goods and services essentially remains the same, but the consumer experience and transaction costs have changed. Mr. Ma's e-commerce innovation brought about not only the change of goods transactions, but also the innovation of the financial system. "Financial babies" have developed along with the e-commerce business model, strongly disrupting the traditional financial system which is built on the monopolistic powers of big banks. It is forcing the financial system to deepen reforms. The jobs created and the logistics services facilitated by Mr. Ma's business model have greatly propelled economic growth. Therefore, innovation of business models is an important part of innovation-driven development.

III. Implementing human resource nurturing strategy to cope with vanishing population dividend

China is a country with a large population and abundant human resources. The negative impacts of the vanishing population dividend can be offset to some degree by extensively developing human resources, raising human resource quality, increasing creativity, and forming a large human resource dividend.

The human resource dividend refers to the increasing proportion of talent with an advanced grasp of humanities, social sciences or natural sciences. It can boost economic growth through the increase of the efficiency of social operation and economic production. The population dividend is reflected chiefly through the decreasing dependency ratio. But the human resource dividend can be acquired by raising the knowledge level of the population, changing the ways of labor, increasing efficiency of labor and management through the use of knowledge and technology. Then, more means of production and consumer goods can be produced with less living labor. The number of people that a worker can support will increase, thereby offsetting the negative impact of the shrinking population dividend to social wealth.

In 2000, the Central Economic Working Conference proposed for the first time to "formulate and implement human resource strategy". In 2001, the *Outline for the 10th Five-Year Plan for Economic and Social Development of the People's Republic of China* devoted a whole chapter to the "implementation of human resource strategy and increase the talent pool". Since its implementation, the government has announced a series of policies and plans regarding the building of the talent force. For example, the project to woo foreign talent has achieved a great deal, along with many other talent projects. However, the strategy still has a lot of problems in practice.

The nurturing and efficient use of talent is a complicated systematic project. China's current human resource strategy focuses on the agglomeration of existing talent, but ignores the nurturing of talent. The current strategy is tentative at best in its effort to utilize talent. It lacks both ambition and concrete policy in the comprehensive nurturing of talent from the very start of childhood.

First, pre-school and primary education is very neglected. Even in Beijing, China's capital, public kindergartens and primary schools fail to fulfil the demand for high-quality education. Many young parents report various difficulties in getting their children into public kindergartens. Primary education has a lot of problems as well. For example, the class size of a typical primary school in Beijing is more than 40, while in America the number is already less than 18 in the Clinton years. Although China's urbanization rate is slowing, the country is still undergoing the process of urbanization. Local governments are overly eager to develop real estate, but often neglect the building of public kindergartens and primary schools.

Second, the household registration system, or hukou, denies children of rural migrant workers the same education opportunity as urban children. The children of these "new urbanites" cannot receive public education in their place of residence. They either have to go to private schools at forbidding costs, or have to drop out very early. This problem is very serious even in Beijing and its surrounding area.

Third, the education industry suffers from excessive commercialization, which overburdens households' human capital investment. In recent years, college graduates suffer from a myriad of difficulties, including unemployment, low wages, and unaffordable housing. Children of low and middle income families have to repay their tuition and buy a house after graduation, reducing them to second-class citizens without social or economic status in cities. They find it hard to marry or make a living, which severely hampers the mental health and growth of the country's talent reserve.

Fourth, current policies often put equipment above people in the use of research funding in universities and research institutions. R&D spending has grown rapidly over the past couple of years, but it focuses mainly on the purchase of equipment over the welfare of researchers. As a result, a lot of funding is wasted on duplicated purchase of equipment, but researchers are denied adequate compensation for their studious effort and innovation. This dampens researchers' enthusiasm for innovation, which in turn causes a lot of equipment to stay idle. The human resource strategy would be hollow if the state fails to rally researchers and fully utilize their potential.

In the face of those problems, a series of measures must be taken in order to truly implement the human resource nurturing strategy.

(1) Cities and affluent rural areas should extensively develop public pre-school and primary education. All children should have the opportunity to receive free public education. Private education should be reserved for high-income families with demand for high-quality education, instead of forcing the poor to enter low-quality private schools.

(2) Improve public primary education in cities, and update regulations regarding class size and faculty-student ratio. The class size for primary schools should be reduced to less than 30 in order to achieve quality education and ensure adequate communication between the teacher and students. In newly developed residential areas and rapidly growing cities, the government should invest in adequate numbers of kindergartens and primary schools. The improvement of pre-school and primary education should be a fundamental part of the human resource nurturing strategy. This can expand the demand for labor in the education system, as well as creating a better environment for the cultivation of talent.

(3) Enlarge the scope of compulsory education and expand financial aid to college students. The current compulsory education system should

be enlarged so as to cover all 12 years of basic education, including intermediate vocational education. Financial aid to college students should also be more generous. Businesses' and individuals' donations for such financial aid should be tax deductible. Tuition repayments and mortgage payments of university graduates should be tax deductible as well, in order to lighten the economic load for young people. Meanwhile, the government should encourage retired people to start enterprises or engage in innovative work in the private sector, and exempt those sources of income from personal income taxes.

(4)   Adjust the management of research funding. State-owned research institutions and universities should have more discretion in their use of non-state-backed research funding. Researchers should be adequately remunerated for their work according to their actual work performance and working hours, which will provide positive incentive for them. The government should allow and encourage researchers to take jobs in businesses, start their own businesses, or receive scientific funding from businesses. In this way the intelligence of researchers can spread further, and research outcomes will materialize faster. The current regulations on research funding are too hollow. For example, the aforementioned *Some Opinions on Improving and Strengthening the Management of Scientific Research Projects and Funding*contains detailed regulations on state funding. But it says little about other sources of funding except that it should be "managed and used according to relevant accounting regulations and the specific demands of donors". In practice, the "relevant accounting regulations" and the "specific demands of donors" differ a great deal or are sometimes even contradictory. This creates great risks for the management and use of funding in "horizontal projects", which takes up a large proportion of the total funding in research institutions and universities. It has become an area where researchers and especially project leaders are prone to mistakes. Future regulations should set

clear boundaries regarding the autonomous powers regarding the use of such funding, so as to avoid too much grey area and embarrassment for researchers.

IV. The circular economy strategy to cope with the vanishing environment dividend

It has been a national strategy since 2005 to develop a circular economy and solve the conflict between high economic growth and resource supply and environmental protection. This has played an important role in the government's attempt to ease the pressure on resource supply and environmental pollution that has come with economic growth. During the 10th Five-Year Plan period and the first four years of the 11th, energy intensity and emissions of SO_2 and COD have significantly declined while the size of the economy doubled. However, with the further development of industrialization and urbanization, China's energy consumption and waste production continues to grow. The resource and environment dividend has vanished.

The development of the circular economy over the past 10 years has achieved much but also faced many problems and pressure. The country has had preliminary success in recycling and reusing materials that are easy or profitable to recycle. But because of the constraints on technological development and market demand, we have faced difficulties in reusing materials that have little to nilo economic benefit in recycling. Since 2013, as economic growth slowed, market competition became fiercer and commodity price fell, domestic demand and prices of recyclable resources have also dropped. Furthermore, rising labor costs and environmental regulation for the recycling industry means that the production costs of recycled resources have shot up. The dual pressure resulted in a continuous slump in the economic benefit of recycling and reusing waste, which has a negative effect on the development of the circular economy.

To cope with the vanishing environment dividend, China should build green civilization and achieve green development under the new normal. It should resolve the conflict between economic growth and environmental constraints, strengthen the development of circular economy, and creatively implement the circular economy strategy. It is an inevitable choice that the circular economy will become the pervasive model for resource utilization and environmental protection.

(i) Improve legislation on circular economy and strengthen its development mechanism

China has passed a series of legislations and policies to promote the circular economy in the past 10 years. The problem now is that these legislations are flawed and some policies change often. This gives uncertainty to the development of circular economy and has a detrimental effect to its development. China should, during the period of the 13th Five-Year Plan, stabilize the legal environment of the circular economy by improving the system of relevant legislations and regulations, so that the circular economy would develop according to law.

(1) Improve and Carry out the Law for the Promotion of the Circular Economy

Since the Law for the Promotion of the Circular economy came into effect in 2009, practice has shown that the piece of legislation played an important role in the development of the circular economy. However, there is a vacuum between the Law for the Promotion of the Circular Economy and the Law for Environmental Protection. The Environmental Protection Law stresses the end-point of environmental protection, i.e. the safe disposal of waste. The Circular Economy Law stresses quantity reduction, reusing, and resources, among which quantity reduction is the priority. The safe disposal of waste stipulated by the Environmental Protection Law is a demand from a substantive legislation, which is binding and enforceable. But the recycle and reuse of resources, which is based on the Circular Economy Law, is merely a nonbinding notion and encouragement. Its main function is more of a declaration of the government's ambition to develop the circular economy, without actual law enforcement power. Therefore, during the 13th Five-Year Plan, the government should consider actually giving the law some substance, and promote it to the same level as the Environmental Protection Law, with a new name of, say, the Law for the Development of the Circular

Economy. The new legislation would include resource exploitation and use, waste management, and recycle and reuse, and have a clear enforcement body.

(2) Formulating some important specialized legislations regarding circular economy

There are a lot of areas that require specialized substantive legislation regarding the circular economy. The 13th Five-Year Plan should put the following aspects as priorities.

First, the formulation of specialized legislation for the promotion of urban garden circular economy.

The building and development of urban garden circular economy is an important part of the promotion of a conservation culture and the major embodiment of this culture in cities. China should develop the urban garden industry in the model of circular economy, and achieve integrated development of the construction of urban gardens and the circular economy. This way, the country can accelerate the promotion of conservation culture in cities, achieve green and circular and low-carbon urban development, and improve the quality of cities. Meanwhile it can also achieve huge economic benefits, raise urban employment, and increase the self-investing ability of the building of urban gardens and conservation culture. But so far, China's urban gardens are managed only as an urban public utility. It focuses too much on the scenery function of these gardens and neglect their ecological and economic ones. As a result, the gardens have become a burden of municipal finance, suffering from underinvestment and underdevelopment. They have become a drag for the urban conservation culture. China has not yet passed any legislation or policy regarding urban gardens and their circular economy. By passing such legislation, the government can stress the legal responsibilities and obligations of municipal governments and citizens in the development of the garden circular economy. The government can also formulate some administrative regulations and tax credits that promote the development of recycling and reusing industry for garden waste.

Second, the formulation of specialized legislation and supporting policies

for agricultural circular economy.

In order to increase yield, China's agricultural industry has excessively used fertilizer and pesticides and engaged in predatory exploitation of the land over the past years. Agriculture has become the main source of surface-source pollution, and is becoming a serious threat to food safety. As agricultural yield grows rapidly, the burning of crops and forest waste has done significant damage and pollution to the environment in both rural areas and cities. Therefore, China should develop circular economy within agriculture, between agriculture and industry, and among agriculture, industry, and the society. This includes the efficient integration of farming, breeding, foresting, animal feed industry, food industry, papermaking, wood board industry, biochemical industry in agriculture (rubber, medicine, etc.), agricultural products deep processing, biofuel, organic fertilizer, bioproducts manufacturing, solar energy, water conservation, recycling and reusing of agricultural waste, ecotourism, and catering services. China should also use scientific fertilizing technology and replace chemical fertilizer and pesticide with organic ones, reducing surface-source pollution. This can not only achieve agricultural growth, but also rapidly develop industries based on agricultural products, increase employment, and accelerate carbon circulation. As a result, agricultural yield will grow, rural income will increase, rural energy will undergo a revolution, food will be of higher quality and safer, carbon will circulate efficiently, the environment will be protected, and climate change will be tackled.

Agriculture is a typical sector with diminishing marginal utility. Its development is usually of a disadvantaged status. China's agricultural land system, based on "household contract responsibility", is beginning to exercise constraint on the efficient and sustainable development of agriculture. The development of agricultural circular economy is also facing difficulties regarding institutions, funding, technology, and industrial organization. The most pressing problems are the following three. Firstly, rural areas, especially the underdeveloped regions, lack big leading businesses that can efficiently integrate and recycle resources.

Decentralized use of land means that inter-farm resource circulation is often hampered by conflicts of interest and moral hazard. It is hard to achieve optimal allocation and large-scale recycling of agricultural resources. Secondly, rural areas lack funding for circular economy projects that have strong scale effects. Otherwise technologically viable models of circular economy cannot be started for lack of money. Thirdly, the land use system based on household contract responsibility has led to much decentralization of land use. It is hard to organically combine circular economy development and the conservation culture to fulfil the "five in one" overall plan for economic, political, cultural, social and ecological progress. Presently some regions have developed some effective circular economy models according to the unique characteristics of the respective regions. China needs to theoretically and practically review these projects, and formulate legislations and policies to promote optimal methods that are suitable to different regions. This has important implications for the promotion of agricultural circular economy and the conservation culture in rural areas.

Third, the formulation of specialized legislation and supporting policies for the circular economy in industrial parks.

Industrial parks are agglomerations of certain industries. It is an optimal industrial structure that improves the benefits of resource agglomeration and economies of scale. It has become the pervasive model for industry layout. However, history shows that if the construction of industrial parks does not conform to the principles of industrial ecology and the methods of circular economy, it may cause industrial businesses to overly concentrate in one area. This kind of area would see high energy and resource consumption and high level of emission and pollution, causing environmental damage to agglomerate. This problem already exists in some regions. Therefore, in the face of these common problems in the development of industrial parks, the government should enact specialized legislation for the circular construction and renovation of industrial clusters. This has important implications for the green, circular, and low-carbon development of the economy in industrial parks.

(ii) Accelerating institutional innovation that indirectly promotes the circular economy

(1) Adopting resource tax system on the circular economy

The price of China's primary resources has been distorted and relatively low. Its costs are largely affected by costs of labor and land, which are continuously rising. High costs and low prices for primary resources mean that the reuse of resources has little economic benefits. This is a major problem facing the development of China's circular economy. Under the new normal, if this problem is not solved through institutional innovation, the sustainability of the circular economy would be affected, and the goal of building a conservation culture would fail to realize. Therefore, it is a priority in the development of circular economy to establish a resource tax system that base resource prices on the compensation of the total cost of resources, including ecological costs. Commodity prices, especially those of resources, have been in decline since 2014, which makes it a golden opportunity now to roll out the resource taxes.

(2) Accelerating the implementation of environmental taxes

Smog has appeared in many places in China since 2013, meaning that China's environment has reached a critical point. However, government regulations of waste emission are only limited to charging some fee for excess emissions. This means that businesses can produce waste for free as long as the total amount is within the predetermined limit. The cost of emission remains too low, reducing the comparative advantage in financial costs of recycling and reusing waste. The regulations fail to press relevant players to recycle resources. It is time to end this model of environmental regulation, for reasons of both the severity of environmental pollution and the unfair distribution of costs of pollution. Therefore, the government should abolish the previous fee-charging system and adopt environmental taxes instead.

(iii) Strengthen financial and tax policies that promotes the circular economy

In many cases, the external benefits exceed internal benefits for firms that are in the circular production and recycling business. Apart from the material products of the circular economy, their main product is actually the reduction of environmental burdens of the society. In this sense, they provide environmental public goods for society. Therefore, the government should subsidize these firms in order to internalize the externalities and incentivize the firms.

First, the government should increase subsidies for recycling and reusing of waste. Based on the urban mineral projects, the government should prioritize subsidies on recycling over the subsidies on waste disposal, and increase subsidies for the recycling and reusing of urban mineral resources. For instance, financial support of recycling solid waste should take precedence over the support of landfills. The cost of landfills should be borne by the producers of waste instead of the state.

Second, the government should publish a list of products and technologies of the circular economy, and prioritize these products in government procurements. People have a natural tendency to buy products made with primary natural resources, which lowers the competitiveness of circular economy products. Therefore, in order to ensure the continuous development of the circular economy during the 13th Five-Year Plan, the government should accelerate the formulation of policies regarding government procurement of circular economy products. It should change the previous rule that the winner is the bidder with lowest prices, and replace it by prioritizing circular economy products. It should also publish a list of these products and technologies.

Third, the government should improve the tax credits for circular economy products. These tax credits appear to reduce the tax base, but on closer look it also reduces the demand for public funding in environmental governance. It changes end-point regulation to preventing waste from its source. In the field of waste recycling, through the state-backed urban mineral projects, the government can implement tax credits under strict regulation in designated urban mineral project areas, integrating the management of mineral projects, material flow, financial subsidies and tax policies. This can increase the efficiency of regulation and significantly reduce the transaction costs for firms to obtain preferential policies. It can also promote the agglomerating development of the waste recycling industry and achieve economies of scale, which is beneficial to the environmental regulations of resource recycling and reduce the risk of secondary pollution.

Fourth, the government should implement extended producer responsibility (EPR). This is a waste disposal system widely used in rich countries. As of 2014, China's EPR system is still in the making. The government has only implemented EPR-like fund systems in a handful of fields including electronic wastes. The income level of China's consumers is relatively low, therefore it is more feasible and fair to adopt producer responsibility instead of consumer responsibility. It can also prevent the injustice that poor people have to bear the responsibility of waste disposal because they consume a lot of second-hand appliances and electrical products. Meanwhile, it is cheaper and incurs less management cost to levy waste disposal charges on businesses than on consumers. During the 13th Five-Year Plan, China should enlarge the rules on electronic waste, and implement EPR as soon as possible on high value consumer products like appliances, rubber and tyre, automobiles, furniture, and mass consumption products like food waste and packaging.

(iv) Improving evaluation and standards for the circular economy

Official standards are an important part of the regulation system. Although China's circular economy already has some technical standards and rules, they are far from meeting the needs of the development of circular economy. The government should formulate standards and improve management of the circular economy, in order to lower the search costs and transaction costs of relevant actors in the circular economy.

(1) Formulating technical standards and rules in the circular economy

The government should research and formulate technical standards and rules on resource utilization as soon as possible, so that the industries can phase out obsolete technologies, prevent secondary pollution, and reduce safety hazards. The government should also pass rules on circular economy products and criteria for market access. It should standardize the quality of recyclable products, ensure product safety, and safeguard consumer interests.

(2) Formulating standards and rules regarding the management of circular economy

According to the stipulation of the *Law for the Promotion of the Circular Economy* and the *Circular Economy Development Strategy and Recent Action Plans*, the government should formulate standards and rules regarding the management of circular economy. These include standards of the designation of circular economy pilot schemes, the formulation and evaluation of plans, and the evaluation of pilot schemes.

(3) Formulating administrative evaluation standards in the circular economy

In order to stimulate the enthusiasm of local governments to develop the circular economy, the government should formulate administrative evaluation standards in the circular economy for different regions. This enables the government to scientifically assess the performance of circular economy in the respective regions.

V. The substantial urbanization strategy to cope with shrinking urbanization dividend

Because of the dual economic system of urban and rural areas, there is a rampant phenomenon of "superficial urbanization" in China, which refers to the fact that a lot of migrant workers work and live in cities but are denied welfare benefits reserved for urban residents. The result is massive waste of land and resources, because the migrant workers cannot and would not forfeit their rural houses and land contracting rights. The urbanization dividend is not fully utilized. The government should accelerate reform on urbanization and the circulation of rural land rights. This will achieve the "urbanization of rights" for migrant workers, increase their purchasing power, increase the scale of land use and the efficiency of agricultural production. This, in turn, can partly offset the shrinking of the urbanization dividend.

(i) The "urbanization of rights" for migrant workers

China has undergone rapid urbanization in the past 10 years. The urbanization rate by residence is 54.77% in 2014. However, because household registration (*hukou*) reform has stalled, the urbanization rate by household registration is only around 35%. Over 270 million migrants live in cities but are denied urban *hukou*. They are stuck in limbo and denied welfare benefits of urban residents such as social security, education for children, and housing benefits. They are constantly worried about their future, and have to save for retirement, children, and healthcare. This kind of urbanization fails to fully utilize its dividend of economic growth. It also raises their savings rate and lowers the consumption rate, which does not help the country's drive to promote economic growth through increasing consumption. Therefore, the government should accelerate the "urbanization of rights" for the existing 270 million migrant workers and the 15 million "new urbanites" that migrate into cities every year. By reducing their worries about retirement, education and healthcare, the savings rate will fall and consumption rate will rise, which can offset to some degree the shrinking of the urbanization dividend.

(ii) Accelerating reform on the transfer of rural land contractual management rights

In November 2014, the State Council published *Some Opinions on Guiding the Orderly Transfer of Rural Land Management Rights and the Reasonable Scale of Agricultural Operation*. This document mandates registration and clarification of rural land management rights, the standardization of their transfer, the regulation of the use of transferred land, and the service and risk management of large-scale land management. We recommend that the State Council leads the Ministry of Agriculture to formulate detailed and viable rules of implementation that guides the orderly transfer of rural land rights. In this process, land management should be effectively integrated with rural real estate, ensuring that the unoccupied houses and homestead can turn into arable land, which can increase the area of arable land. The government should take measures to prevent land grab and the illegal development of real estate on rural land.

(iii) Facilitate the integration of land rights transfer and new-type urbanization

Land transfer can be combined with the development of small town clusters in qualified areas, especially in the surroundings of counties and big towns, so that rural areas and small towns can together achieve green, circular and low-carbon development. These places can exchange urban housing for rural land rights. The government and urban real estate developers can cooperate to buy rural land rights with adequate consultation of and consent from farmers. Then, after the arrangement of land, the government and real estate developers can bid for large-scale operating agencies (or individuals that have the ability), and perform large-scale production on the land using green, circular, and low-carbon development methods. They should also prioritize the recruitment of original land holders to be employed in the new, large-scale agriculture.

VI. The manufacturing and emerging industries upgrading strategy to cope with vanishing structural dividend

Slowing of growth in heavy industry has caused the structural dividend to vanish. The fundamental way to deal with it is to accelerate the development of new industries and the upgrade of manufacturing. In the Report on the Work of the Government in 2015, Premier Li Keqiang proposed the "Made in China 2025" initiative that promotes innovation, smart transformation, strengthening the foundation, and green development. It aims to transfer China from a manufacturer of quantity to a manufacturer of quality. Meanwhile, it also proposed the plan of "Internet Plus". These two plans include the development of emerging manufacturing industry and the upgrade and transformation of traditional industries by using smart technology. It is the embodiment of China's grand strategy of integration of industrialization and digitization under the new normal. Future manufacturing and emerging industry will develop in the direction of "Internet+service" and "Internet+manufacturing".

(i) Nurturing the development of strategic emerging industries

Strategic emerging industries are the deep integration of emerging technologies and emerging industries. They are the emerging power engine of economic growth in the post-industrialization age. It is an important tool to cope with the slowing growth in traditional industries, the vanishing structural dividend, the implementation of innovation-driven development strategy, and the nurturing of new economic opportunities under the new normal. In 2010, the State Council made a decision to "accelerate the nurturing and development of strategic emerging industries", implemented plans to facilitate their development, and made significant progress. "Made in China 2025" and "Internet Plus" will become the main technological path in guiding the development of strategic emerging industries.

(1) Strengthening breakthroughs in core technologies

China has made breakthroughs in a lot of strategic emerging industries, leading the world in high-end equipment technologies such as high-speed railway and the integrated development of its system, maritime equipment, new generation information technology, and electric cars. However, in the seven designated strategic emerging industries, many of China's core technologies still rely heavily on multinationals in developed countries. The industries and their key products have not broken their technological monopoly, or even facing technological blockade. And there have not yet been a breakthrough in high-end carbon fiber, graphene, integrated circuit chips, smart manufacturing, biomedical products, and seeds. Therefore, China should concentrate its energy and break the technology blockade, which is crucial to the development of strategic emerging industries. It should also conduct institutional innovation and nurture a group of strategic leading enterprises that have strong innovative ability. It should devote effort to the integrated application and commercialization of technologies, and strive to form large-scale production systems that are internationally competitive.

(2) Optimizing and integrating the policy system

In order to accelerate the development of strategic emerging industries, China has implemented a series of supporting policies, including the previous policies that support high-tech industries. But practice shows that there are still some problems waiting to be solved. The most striking problem is that there are too many government departments in charge of policymaking and enforcement in this area. It is difficult to concentrate in a single direction. Strategic emerging industries cover a lot of fields and involves a lot of government offices, including the National Development and Reform Commission, Ministry of Finance, Ministry of Industry and Information Technology, Ministry of Commerce, Ministry of Science and Technology, and the State Taxation Administration. Some policies have clear marks of the departments that issue them. Some are even conflicting and contradictory to each other. Therefore, it is necessary to implement further reform and conduct a thorough review of previous policies regarding the development of emerging industries, and to combine similar policies, coordinate between differing policies, and form a clear, consistent, easily enforceable policy set.

(3) Improve investment and financing in emerging industries

One common feature of emerging industries is their potential for efficient and rapid growth. However, because their technology, products and business models are all new, they face an uncertain and highly risky market. Therefore, emerging industries face a lot of difficulties in investment and financing. In order to accelerate their development, the State Council decided on Jan 4, 2015 to combine the central strategic emerging industry specialized fund and the central infrastructure investment fund. This will attract leading enterprises, capable financial corporations and private capital to cooperate and establish a national emerging industries investment guiding fund. This fund will have an annual investment of 40 billion yuan, devoted to supporting the financing of startup firms in emerging industries. It will promote the combination of technology and market, innovation and entrepreneurship, and incubation and cultivation. However, strategic emerging industries cover a lot of areas and need huge amounts of investment. The annual 40 billion yuan is far from enough to fulfil this demand.

Further channels are needed to attract capital to these industries. Especially, the government should boost financial innovation and coordinate it with fiscal policies, using government discount and procurement to enlarge the market of emerging industries and lower their risk and cost of financing.

(4) Deepening reform on economic management and create more market space

It is essential to deepen reform on economic system and management, crack down on industry monopolies and their fiefdoms, eliminate barriers of entry of new products in strategic emerging industries like new energy, green vehicles, internet, biomed, and medical equipment. For instance, in the process of integration of China's telecom, broadcasting, and internet networks, the introduction of private capital can increase network efficiency and lower the cost of information infrastructure investment, accelerating the innovation and development of the internet industry. Development of new energy industry can be accelerated by management reform on electricity, developing distributed network of new energy, and solving the problem of connecting new energy to the grid. The government should also reform the market access and product circulation in medicine, especially the market for domestically produced medical equipment. This can facilitate the entry of these equipment into the domestic medical market, significantly lowering the cost of healthcare in China.

(5) Protecting intellectual property and smoothing the commercialization of scientific research

The protection of intellectual property is an important foundation of the development of emerging industries. The commercialization of scientific research is also an important part. China needs to build a protection system for intellectual property to safeguard the interest of innovators. It is an intrinsic demand of strategic emerging industries to strengthen the commercialization system for scientific research.

First, the government should strengthen enforcement of intellectual property laws. China has already passed a series of laws and regulations on intellectual property protection, and established intellectual property courts. But in practice, the country lacks a cultural atmosphere that respects intellectual property. Pirate products are rife, and intellectual property are frequently infringed. It is hard to protect legitimate interests, obtain evidence, and enforce relevant regulations. The cost of rights protection is also high. The main reason is that there are too many departments in charge of intellectual protection. There is insufficient coordination between the various laws, administrative regulations and policies. The legal system for intellectual property protection should be perfected, with the focus put on enforcement. Meanwhile, the government should also train personnel in the enforcement of intellectual property laws.

Second, the commercialization of scientific research should be strengthened. Apart from protecting intellectual property rights, China should also smooth the spread and application of scientific research, accelerate its transformation to production forces, and promote the development of emerging industries. The government should create suitable conditions for the commercialization of scientific research. On the one hand, the cooperation between industry, education, and research should be strengthened, combining the R&D activity of research institutions and the demands of businesses, so that scientific research can be directly commercialized into technological innovation. On the other hand, the government should develop intermediary services in science and technology, perfect relevant regulations, establish platforms for these services, lower the search cost and transaction cost of scientific research, and provide high quality services to the commercialization of scientific research in strategic emerging industries.

(ii) Pushing the transformation and upgrade of traditional industries

China is still undergoing the process of industrialization and urbanization. The production capacity of traditional resource-oriented heavy industry is approaching the market ceiling. Traditional functional products and process manufacturing are also entering a stage of surplus. China has become a big manufacturer in quantity. However, the technological level and product quality of China's traditional manufacturing is still low. International competitiveness of these sectors is dismal, except a handful of advanced industries such as high-speed railway. Therefore, China is largely at the low end of the "smiling curve" on the international value chain. In order to cope with the slowing growth of manufacturing under the new normal, China should accelerate the upgrade of its traditional industries and increase their competitiveness.

In the Report on the Work of the Government in 2015, Premier Li Keqiang proposed the "Made in China 2025" plan that emphasizes the upgrade of manufacturing industries. This plan focuses on advanced manufacturing and high-end equipment. It aims to nurture emerging advanced industries like smart manufacturing, as well as accelerating the upgrade of traditional manufacturing. Policies are being carried out that guide the efficient allocation of resources in advanced manufacturing, high-tech industries and strategic emerging industries to occupy the high ground and increase manufacturing efficiency and competitiveness. The aim is to inject a smart element into "Made in China", accelerating the country's transformation from a large economy in size into a large economy in strength.

In order to transform and upgrade traditional manufacturing industries, the key is to create a suitable institutional and policy environment and facilitate the reorganization within traditional industries.The industries should also introduce competition mechanism, realize breakthrough in key technologies, achieve the integrated application and innovation of material, manufacturing, and information technology, and develop high-end smart products.

The government's task in this aspect is to pick vital industries and nudge businesses to increase their drive of transformation and upgrade. In the field of primary manufacturing, the government should increase the introduction and integrated innovation of information technology. China is the world's largest manufacturer and user of lathe, but China's core technology in this field still relies on import. Other fields with similar problems include automobile, shipbuilding, engineering machinery, and maritime machinery. Therefore, major efforts should be devoted to these fields in which China has advantage in material manufacturing but lacks the core technologies, achieving "Made in China" of the whole equipment. Processing industries such as steel, chemicals, building materials, nonferrous metal, and cement should focus on key technologies of energy conservation, environmental protection, clean production, and waste recycling, in order to achieve a clean upgrade of traditional raw material heavy industries. In the field of electronics and information technology, the industries should develop smart products and focus on brand building, transforming the industries from pirate makers to original innovators. They should also utilize the "Internet Plus" strategy and transform China's traditional service sector into a new model based on information technology and networking.

VII. The trade in services improvement strategy to cope with shrinking net export dividend

China is the world's biggest trader. Although China's export and import dependence has declined from its peak in 2007, but its trade dependence (measured by trade as % of GDP)is still more than 60%. More than 180 million people are employed in trade-related sectors. Trade also accounts for 18% of tax revenue, playing an important role in economic growth.

Under the new normal, China's trade growth has slowed. The net export dividend is gradually vanishing, exerting a drag on economic growth. The fundamental reason is that there is a severe structural imbalance in China's imports and exports. There is a trade surplus in goods and manufacturing, but a huge deficit in services. According to data from the Ministry of Commerce[1], growth in China's import in services exceeds growth in service exports, and the trade deficit in services keeps growing. In 2014, the size of China's trade in services reached $604.3 billion, a growth by 12.6% from 2013 and the first time this figure exceeds $600bn. Total value of import is $222.21bn, an increase of 7.6%.

---

1 Unless otherwise specified, data of China's trade in services are from *China Statistics on Trade in Services 2014*, published by the China Commerce and Trade Press.

Total value of export is $382.13bn, an increase of 15.8%. The trade deficit in services is a whopping $159.9bn, making China the country with the biggest such deficit in the world.

Under the new normal, the growth of trade in goods and manufacturing has slowed or even reversed. China's net export will continuously shrink, which will drag down economic growth. Therefore, China should implement the trade in services improvement strategy and increase support for trade in services. The most important way out of the shrinking net export dividend is to achieve the balanced development of trade in goods and services.

(i) Formulating a strategic plan for improvement of trade in services

Trade in services involves a lot of government departments, including commerce, foreign affairs, development and reform, culture and education, finance and insurance, tourism, industrialization, information technology, quality regulation, and customs. We suggest that the State Council lead the formulation of China's service in trade improvement strategy based on the 2015 official document *Some Opinions on Accelerating the Development of Trade in Services*. This strategic plan should also be included in the *Outline for the 13rd Five-Year Plan for Economic and Social Development*.

(ii) Bolstering the weak and Consolidating the Strong in Service Trade

The reasons are complicated as to why the development of China's trade in services has lagged behind. First, China's service sector is relatively backward, with few "products" fit for export, especially in areas with low international competitiveness such as finance, insurance, creative design, intellectual property, culture and education. Second, trade in services covers a lot of sectors and involves a lot of government departments, making it hard to coordinate and communicate. Third, there are many non-tariff barriers in the international trade in services. China's legal system for trade in services is still flawed. It fails to adequately regulate and protect trade in services. Fourth, there is regional inequality in the development of trade in services, which needs more opening up and cooperation.

Considering both the advantaged and disadvantaged industries of trade in services, China should formulate supporting measures based on the trend of international development of trade in services. It should support the weak industries to enlarge their scale and shrink trade deficit. It should also support the strong industries in their quest to consolidate their strength and develop China's distinct brands in services.

First, the "Exploring China" initiative should be implemented. Tourism is an industry where China has resource advantages and strong international competitiveness. It also makes up a large proportion of trade in services. In 2014, China's export in tourism makes up 24.5% of total export in services. But meanwhile, tourism is also the industry where the trade deficit in services is the largest, marking up 64% of the total deficit. The "Exploring China" initiative will improve the material and institutional environment of China's tourism. It will promote China's tourism resources and attract international organizations to hold global exhibitions and events in China. The country should nurture high value tourism products like skiing and mountain climbing, forming renowned Chinese brands of tourism. Then, China's advantages in tourism will be consolidated, and trade deficit in this industry will decline.

Second, the "Overseas Promotion of Chinese Culture" initiative should be implemented. The Chinese traditional culture is very rich and profound. China's modern culture has also made a lot of progress, making the country a great power in culture and sports. However, China still fails to adequately develop its cultural soft power. It lacks influential cultural products and reputation. China should build its soft power and implement the "Overseas Promotion of Chinese Culture" initiative to encourage the cultural export of Chinese traditional and modern cultural products, broadcasting, TV and film, publishing, and the internet, in order to nurture advantages in these emerging service sectors.

Third, China should increase its export of financial services. Over the past 10 years, the trend in contemporary trade in services is that trade in finance and insurance has grown a lot faster than traditional sectors. The global trade superpowers, such as the U.S. and the U.K., are all strong exporters of financial and insurance services. Take the U.K. as a typical example. The value of its trade in services ranks the 4th in the world, but its export in services ranks the 2nd, making up 6.3% of the world's total export in services. Finance and insurance services is the most important part of the United Kingdom's trade in services, whose export makes up 30% of the country's total export in services. But China's export in finance and insurance is no match to its might in goods and manufacturing trade. Although finance is among the fastest growing sector in China's export in services, it still only accounts for 3.3% of China's total export in services in 2013. Therefore, China should coordinate the establishment of international financial centers in Shanghai and Shenzhen as well as the Belt and Road initiative, and bolster the export of financial services with adequate regulation of risks.

Fourth, China should increase its export of technology. With the development of service contracting, computing and information technology is China's strength in service exports and also where trade deficit is large. China has also gained international competitiveness in e-commerce, data centers, technological services, and technology licensing. China should implement the technology exporting initiative. It should consolidate the strengths in service outsourcing in IT services, and increase its support of the export of the aforementioned knowledge-intensive services. The country should also bolster the development and export of equipment that support financial and technological services, and facilitate the "servitization" of manufacturing. This is an important way to boost technology exports.

Fifth, China should increase its support for export in the logistics industry. Transport and logistics makes up a large proportion in China's trade in services, with the second largest trade deficit after tourism in China's service sectors. China is world's biggest trader in goods, so it is abnormal that China's trade in logistical services is still in deficit. Therefore, China should develop policy measures that support trade in goods, and bolster the export of transporting services.

(iii) Setting up pilot schemes of service trade innovation

China should review its existing pilot innovations related to trade in services, and select qualified cities, industrial parks, free trade zones or border economic cooperation zones, and designate some of them as pilot schemes for innovation in service trade. These pilot schemes should improve its mechanism for attracting talent and explore new models of trade in services. They should loosen investment and technological regulations and entry barriers in high-end service sectors such as finance, insurance, telecommunication, aviation, and e-commerce. They should implement "black list" systems that allow trade in all areas outside the list instead of approving trade only in a designated white list. They should also phase out regulations that are not transparent, and improve policies in export guarantee and financing of small and middle businesses. They can explore innovation in financing such as using intellectual property as collateral. Furthermore, these pilot schemes can experiment in trade export in special custom regulation zones and bonded areas, explore innovations in trade convenience, and increase the agglomeration and innovation ability in service trade resources.

(iv) Accelerating the opening up of service sectors

Before the full implementation of the aforementioned "black list" system of foreign investment, China should first facilitate bilateral free-trade agreement in services with main trade partners and Belt and Road countries. It should actively participate in regional economic cooperation and multilateral and bilateral negotiations in order to enlarge the space for the development of trade in services. China should also strive to form economic zones with advantages in services in trade, which can coordinate with trade in goods. Furthermore, it should increase its participation in the making of global rules regarding trade in services.

(v) Accelerating institutional reform and innovation regarding trade in services

China should review its regulation system of trade in services. It should accelerate the amendment of the Foreign Trade Law, clarify the legal responsibilities and trade order that reflects the characteristics of trade in services, and improve relevant legislation in important service departments. China should accelerate its introduction of value-added tax (VAT) and improve tax policies in order to promote service export. It should improve its statistics of trade in services and revise the statistic indices. Meanwhile, the commerce departments should increase cooperation with statistics and foreign exchange departments to establish a comprehensive system for the statistics, monitoring, operation and analysis of the development of trade in services. An emergency safeguarding mechanism in service trade should also be established and perfected.

References

1. Li, Yang. "The new normal of China's economy is different from that of the world." *People's Daily*, 12 Mar 2015.

2. Ma, Guangyuan. "A comprehensive and accurate understanding of the new normal of China's economy." *Economic Information Daily*, 10 Nov 2014.

3. Wang, Songqi. "The origin of the 'new normal'." *The Chinese Banker*, 9 (2014).

4. Li, Yang. "Increasing quality and efficiency to adapt to the economic new normal." *People's Daily*, 11 Jun 2014.

5. Cai, Fang. *Beyond Demographic Dividend*. Social Science Academic Press, 2011.

6. Cai, Fang. "Preparing for the Lewis turning point and utilize the demographic dividend." http://finance.eastmoney.com/news/1350,2010092297420977.html

7. Long, Buhai. "Breaking the double constraint of savings and foreign exchange: a review of Chenery's two-gap model." *Economic Review*, 2 (1992): 48-51.

8. Qin, Wanshun, and Aiguo Tang. "The two-gap model and foreign investment." *Economic Science* 19.6 (1997): 32-37.

9. Wang, Xin. "On the shortage of migrant workers." *China Statistics* 10 (2004):29-30.

10. Wang, Xuebin. "The causes and solutions of migrant worker shortage." *World Economic Outlook* 18 (2005): 26-29.

11. Lin, Justin. "What is the economic new normal." *Insight China*, Oct 2014.

12. Zhang, Huilian, and Hongju Wang. "The meaning of economic new normal." *The Chinese Banker* 6 (2014): 10-13.

13. Xiang, Songzuo. "The new normal of China's economy." *Talents*, 6 (2014).

14. Liu, Shijin. "The Chinese economy under the new normal of growth." *China Development Observation* 4 (2014): 17-18.

15. Guo, Ticheng, and Xinxin Kong. "China is entering a period of scientific talent dividend." *Hongqi Wengao*, Jun 2013.

16. Qi, Jianguo. "The context of China's economic new normal." *West Forum* 1 (2015).

17. Qi, Jianguo. "The connotation and mechanism of China's economic new normal." *Economic Review* 1 (2015).

18. Qi, Jianguo. "Circular Economy and Green Development: Calling for the Fourth Technological Revolution." *Economic Review* 1 (2013).

19. Qi, jianguo, and Jingjing Liang. "On the social welfare effect of innovation-driven development." *Economic Review* 8 (2013).

20. Li, Gang. "China's trade in services: a bright spot in development transition." China Forex Magazine 6 (2014): 74-75.

21. Hong, Yinxing: "On the strategy of innovation-driven development." *Economist(China)*, 1 (2013).

22. Zhang, Laiming. "The scientific and theoretic meaning of the Chinese economic new normal." *Economic Review* 1 (2015).

23. Zhao, Zhenhua. "Common misunderstandings of China's economic new normal and their explanations." *Economic Review* 1 (2015).

This book is the result of a co-publication agreement between China Social Sciences Press (China) and Paths International Ltd (UK)

This book is published with financial support from China Classics International (经典中国国际出版工程)

Title: The New Normal of China's Economy: Connotation and Measurement
By Institute of Quantitative &Technical Economics, Chinese Academy of Social Sciences
Translated by Wang Pinda
ISBN: 978-1-84464-579-4
Ebook ISBN: 978-1-84464-580-0

Paths International Ltd
www.pathsinternational.com
Published in the United Kingdom

CPSIA information can be obtained
at www.ICGtesting.com
Printed in the USA
LVHW101003170620
658094LV00006B/107

9 781844 645794